An End of Innocence

About the Book

Three youths canoeing down the rapids of the Colorado find greater peril in a so-called civilized town near the river than in its savage waters. Each youth is different from the others, but all are close friends, and when one is framed by townspeople, the others go to his aid. They find their greatest ally in a lovely girl. Suspensefully and dramatically the popular writer Donald Honig tells a story of the young pitted against prejudices and evil stemming from times past.

An End of
Innocence

by Donald Honig

G.P. Putnam's Sons
New York

For My Nephew
George Honig

An End of Innocence

Chapter I

We were riding a slow current between low sandstone cliffs. Up ahead, where the river widened, I could see the bright morning sun winking on the waves. The canoe was following the water with ease and smoothness, and we were hardly using our paddles at all, except to guide ourselves.

Farther down we passed some pebbly shoreline that looked like a good place to stop for lunch, but it was still too early for that. The cliff lines on either side of us became lower and more sunshine poured into the great canyon of the Colorado River. Looking ahead, I could see some cottonwoods growing right out on the edge of some of the ridges, their green leaves bright against the red rock of the cliffs.

I was in the stern. Bruce was sitting midship, stroking softly at the water; the paddle looked like so much balsa in his powerful black hands. Fox was in the bow. He was there because he had the most experience. He had spent parts of previous summers canoeing on Lake Champlain and on lakes and rivers in New England. The man in the bow does the steering—a pretty tricky job when you're canoeing a river like the Colorado. Neither Bruce nor I had ever done much more on water than sit in a rowboat in Central Park.

We were riding a flat-bottomed, seventeen-footer of aluminum alloy, which we had chipped in for and bought on Fox's recommendation. It was durable and unsinkable as well as lighter than a wooden canoe, and this was important because when you came to places where you could not follow the water, you had to portage—which is a fancy word for taking your canoe out of the water and carrying it around the really rough places on the river until you could put it in again.

The Colorado had lots of surprises to offer. Great stretches of calm and almost noiseless water could suddenly be followed by a series of rapids that went like torrents through treacherous rocks that could easily capsize you if you weren't careful.

But for the moment we were riding calm water, and there are few things more pleasurable than taking a good canoe over friendly water.

Bruce turned around and grinned at me.

"Don't fall asleep back there," he said.

I could have, too, it was so quiet. The only sound was that of the small waves slapping against the sides of the canoe—they make just a bit more noise against the aluminum canoes than they do the wooden ones; that's what Fox said, anyway. But he said, too, that only somebody who's had lots of experience in a wooden canoe would know it. To me, with my grand inexperience, the sounds were like part of the quiet.

Then I began to notice a change in the water. It was moving faster. The sandstone cliffs were beginning to pass faster too. The current was picking up, was beginning to run with a strong and willful ease, as if it had been turned loose. I could feel the building strength under the canoe. Bruce turned around.

"Rapids," he said.

We exchanged serious looks, then grinned at each other. This wouldn't be the first time since we'd started out a few days ago that we would be going over the white water, but I still wasn't used to it. I wondered if you ever got used to it. I felt that strange mixture of fear and excitement; this was, after all, what we had come nearly two thousand miles for—to follow the Colorado as far as we could. We had been warned about the rapids and the waterfalls and the rocks. It seemed to us an opportunity for high adventure—there were few of these opportunities left today —and I felt it would be reasonable and understandable to be a little afraid. In fact, I think it's probably a good thing, especially when you're challenging a force like the Colorado River. You're not going to get cocky and take foolish chances. A sense of fear is sometimes a good weight to have in the pit of your stomach.

There was no question about it now. The current was really moving with a sweep and a run. And we were going with it, streaking along, the canoe riding low in the water because of our weight and that of our gear. Now and then some water leaped over the sides of the canoe and splashed inside. Some of the back spray was hitting me in the face along with the cool, clear wind.

Then we could hear it up ahead, murmurous at first, but getting louder, building into a soft, familiar roaring. I could see Fox working harder in the bow, making sure we steered clear of the rocks. There was an almost weightless feeling now as we shot ahead over the swift water that was brawling and roaring around us and beating itself into foam around the rocks. The canyon walls seemed to be flashing by.

The bow leaped out of the water for a moment, then struck down again and shot forward like an arrow. We were well clear of the rocks, which was a good thing. One thought stayed right to the very front of my mind whenever we were riding the rapids: in the event we turn over, don't try to swim to shore, but stick with the canoe. But we weren't going to capsize; not in these waters, anyway. They felt too good and free and fast. They were tumbling and roaring over the rocks and blowing spray into our faces and leaping into the canoe and carrying us along at somewhere between fifteen and twenty miles an hour.

Last winter we had packed our skis and taken a bus out to this part of the country and skied the slopes around Aspen. This morning I had thought of those snows melting all spring and summer and running down the mountain slopes into the brooks, which run into the creeks, which flow eventually into various small rivers, which pour into the Colorado, which empties finally a thousand miles later into the Gulf of California. So, if you wanted to think about it, we were now riding the same snows over which we had swept down the mountain slopes last winter; those same snows carrying our canoe along as they found their way home to the sea.

Then we were past the rocks and the current began to slow. I could feel the water's terrific energy beginning to ease, like a runaway horse beginning to tire. The roaring was behind us now, the sound softening on my ears. The hissing white foam was no longer around the canoe. The tension went out of my arms and shoulders and back as a great relaxation set in.

"We're through it!" I yelled.

Fox, in the bow, half turned around. I could see his nose sticking out from under the bill of his baseball cap.

"What?" he called.

"He says we're through it," Bruce said.

"Ask him how he can tell," Fox said.

Bruce turned around. Tiny jets of water were shining on his rugged black face.

"Steve," he said, "Fox wants to know how you can tell."

Wise guys.

It was suddenly very quiet again. The water was rocking against the sides of the canoe. I was getting hungry now but didn't say anything about it. Whenever Bruce or I said we were hungry, Fox would say it wasn't time to stop yet, that we could cover more distance. That's because we had elected him captain and I guess he felt the need to show us he had the most endurance.

I knew we were going to stop soon, though. We were planning to camp out for a day or so in this area, which was somewhere near the Colorado-Utah line. We planned to do this every so often, setting up camp along the river and then hiking and looking around a bit. We would be pulling in soon because we had been told about a good campsite nearby and because it was near a town, according to our maps. This would give us a chance to stock up on food again, because as we went farther down the canyon into Utah we would be going through some pretty lonely country.

Then Fox gave us the signal to start paddling toward shore. There was a point here where the cliffs broke away and there were grassy clearings shaded by stands of pine and spruce. With the town nearby, this seemed like a perfect place to camp . . . which shows that you can never tell. Little did we know all the things that lay in store for us before we would be able to put our canoe back into the water.

Chapter II

We decided in April to make the trip. We had enjoyed Colorado so much when we'd been out there skiing that we felt we wanted to see that part of the world at another time of year. A canoe trip sounded like the best and most inexpensive way to do it. The fact that I had no experience in a canoe made it sound even more interesting. This is called by some people the spirit of youth and by others insanity. My friends warned me that I was likely to get smashed up on the rocks, drowned or go to oblivion over a waterfall. But such heavy warnings can hardly bother a fellow who's sitting in a nice, dry, warm dormitory room.

Come spring and everybody starts talking about summer. Some people were planning to go to Europe to hike or bike, while others were going to get jobs and earn some money, and still others were going to just plain loaf.

Bruce, Fox and I were roommates in a New England college. We were only freshmen, but we all had a nice sense of self-importance—that special kind of self-importance that only freshmen can feel. It comes mostly from seeing how unimportant you are in a large university. To make our trip sound less like a purely good time, we told people that we were going to make certain ecological studies as we went along. We really planned to do that, too, since we all were interested in that sort of thing.

Bruce was particularly looking forward to the trip. He had been brought up in a New York ghetto and, maybe because of denial, had developed a real poet's love for nature and the outdoors. He was a big strong guy, and to hear him talk about his feelings for trees and flowers and natural life was most interesting. At first he had planned to work over the summer to earn some money, but his family insisted he take the trip and have the opportunity to see all those things while he was still young and had the chance. So he compromised. He said he would join us since we were going to be away for four weeks, which would allow him to spend the first half of the summer on the trip, then work the second half. He had been promised a job teaching ghetto kids basketball. He was a good-natured guy, quiet, with a sly sense of humor and a lot of pride.

Fox was a different sort. Foxcroft Rayson Huntington. One third of his friends called him Hunt, another third called him Ray, and the rest called him Fox. We called him Fox because he seemed to like that the least. He came from a rich, old family in Massachusetts. They had been in the country for so long that you got the feeling his ancestors had been there to greet the *Mayflower*.

Fox was a sort of fussy guy who liked things just so.

His bed was always neat and his clothes always hung up very neatly. He wasn't the best pupil in school and had to work hard to keep his grades respectable, but he had a much higher opinion of his mind than the professors seemed to. Fox called any professor who gave him low marks "uninformed."

He'd had what was called a privileged childhood, going off to summer camp, which was where he had learned to handle a canoe. He knew just how to load a canoe so that the weight was at dead center, how to steer through white water, and things like that. He was a strong swimmer. He also knew a lot about camping out.

Now and then he would criticize the match of your jacket and pants, but he really was all right. He'd never hesitate to lend you money or to give of his time if he thought he could help.

The first time his parents came to visit he happened to be out of the room. I'll never forget their look of surprise when they saw Bruce there (Fox hadn't told them he was rooming with a black guy). Now, Bruce can be pretty sly when he wants to. He noticed the looks of surprise on the faces of Mr. and Mrs. Huntington, and he got up from his chair to greet them.

"My name is Bruce Price," he said, shaking hands with Mr. Huntington. "This is Steve Miller," he said, gesturing toward me. Too lazy to get up, I just waved.

Neither of the Huntingtons said anything.

"The reason Fox asked me to room with him," Bruce said, "is because he's prejudiced. He doesn't like

Negroes, you see, and in order to try and get over this, he asked me to room with him." Then Bruce stepped back, hung his thumbs in his belt and stared at the people.

The Huntingtons didn't know what to say. They were a nice-looking couple, middle-aged, well-dressed, with bright, wintry looks to them. The father had what looked like a five-dollar haircut—the kind of haircut where the barber doesn't interrupt your thoughts with aimless chatter, and, when he does talk, he calls you "sir." Mr. Huntington spoke up first.

"My son doesn't have a prejudiced bone in his body," he said.

"He wasn't brought up that way," Mrs. Huntington said. "We brought him up to respect every race, color and creed."

"If he has any prejudices," the father said, jabbing the air with his finger to make his point, "then he acquired them right here in this school."

The mother nodded her head firmly to that.

"We're proud that he's rooming with a Negro," the father said.

"I'm glad to hear that," Bruce said.

"We couldn't be happier," the mother said.

Later that night, after the Huntingtons had gone, we were sitting around the room having a beer.

"You know something," Fox said. He was sitting in a chair, his leg draped over the armrest, a can of beer in his hand. "I frankly thought I might get some flak from my parents because I'm rooming with a black.

They're kind of conservative and old-fashioned you know. But all through dinner they never said a word about it."

"You see," Bruce said. "You never can tell about people."

So that was Bruce and that was Fox. There we were—two guys from the sidewalks of New York and one from the lush old shade of comfortable New England. On the surface, we were probably an unlikely trio, but somehow we all managed to hit it off. We liked the same brand of beer, the same writers, the same movies; but the main thing we had in common was a love for the outdoors. We did a lot of hiking in the hills around the school and went skiing whenever we could.

So when it came to planning the trip, we went at it with a lot of excitement. At the end of June we began gathering together our gear. We chipped in for the canoe, tied it to the roof of our rented car and set out for the West, looking forward to a month of adventure.

We had read all the books on the subject that we could lay our hands on. The first man to lead an expedition down the Colorado was a one-armed Civil War veteran named John Wesley Powell. In the spring of 1869 he led ten men on what was then a one-thousand-mile voyage into the unknown. Powell and his men had to face not just the rapids, but also the threat of unfriendly Indians and hunger and other problems. We read his account of his journey and it

17

really fired us up. We were looking forward to lots of adventure on the river. We had plenty of that all right, but the real adventure on the trip was going to come on land. And it was something that we could hardly have expected.

Chapter III

We dragged the canoe out of the water and set it in the grass. Then we began to unload our gear. Bruce and I did that while Fox looked around for a good place to pitch our tent and make camp. He was always very serious about this and regarded the selection of a campsite with the same deep concern as if he were planning to build a house on the spot.

First he would find some level ground. He would always get kind of dramatic about finding the place. "Here," he'd say, tapping the ground with his foot. "Here's where we spend the night." Then he'd get to work smoothing the ground—and I mean smoothing it. Every twig and pebble had to be swept away before he would put down the waterproof tarp. Then the tent went up.

Bruce, who claimed he knew how to cook, was in charge of setting up the fold-up stove. His cooking tasted pretty bad the first few days, but after that it seemed to improve. Either he got better or else our taste buds got the message that this was going to be the food for the next few weeks and surrendered the memory of better cooking. Fox then decided which way the prevailing winds were blowing and told Bruce which way to face the stove so we wouldn't get the smoke in our faces. Whenever we did get the smoke in our faces, Fox was quick to say the wind had changed, while we were quick to say that he had made a mistake.

Once we had the basics set up, Fox then handed out the assignments, such as gathering wood and digging a garbage pit and a latrine. One thing that we all took very seriously was keeping a neat camp and not leaving behind any kind of a mess. We always made sure to bury our garbage and then cover the spot with rocks and logs so that animals wouldn't come sniffing around and dig it up. You learn a great respect for the wilderness and don't want to do anything to deface it. You come to realize how one empty beer can or one piece of paper can really spoil the look of an otherwise beautiful spot. You can hit a site where a hundred camps have been before you, but, if there's no sign of anything left behind, you can still have that great feeling of being the first one ever to be there, which is part of the fun and excitement of camping.

Bruce then went to work and cooked a pretty good lunch of soup and beans and carrots and strong coffee.

"Your cooking is improving," Fox said.

"I think it's your taste that's improving," Bruce said.

"I think it's the food," I said. "It's too good even for Bruce to spoil."

"Of course you have to remember that you work up a pretty good appetite canoeing," Fox said, stretching out on the grass, holding his tin cup of coffee. "You get so hungry that even a rock would taste good."

"I'll try that for dinner," Bruce said. "I'll cook a rock."

"Actually the beans tasted a bit pebbly," I said.

"Well," Bruce said, "I don't want you fellows to get too fat. I don't want the canoe sinking in the middle of the river."

"Did you ever notice," Fox said, "that no matter where you go, from the best restaurant to the lowliest diner, the chef is always temperamental?"

"It's true," I said.

"Someday I'll get a compliment from you guys," Bruce said, pretending resentment.

"We eat your grubby cooking," Fox said. "That's compliment enough."

"You eat or you starve, man," Bruce said.

This went on after every meal, three times a day.

Later we hiked around for an hour or so. Bruce pointed out to us all kinds of wild flowers, like blue violets and buttercups and yellow goldenrod and sunflowers. There were great sheets of them spread softly across the meadows and hillsides. Bruce insisted on describing them all to us, when they bloomed, how long they lasted, over what parts of the country and in what kind of locations they grew, and things like that. He had this great and genuine fondness for flowers and all the other things of nature. And he had got it all out of books, because here was a child of the city who hadn't ever seen more than Central Park until he'd gone away to college.

Fox was a big authority on woodchucks and chipmunks and animals like that, and on the way back to camp he bent our ears about them. He told us how the woodchuck hibernated underground all winter, how its body temperature went down to something like 40 or 50 degrees and how it would just lie there all winter, barely breathing or eating or anything, until it revived again in the spring.

"That's how Bruce sits in class all winter," I said.

I wasn't an authority on anything out there. I couldn't tell a woodchuck from a mountain lion. I was just a history major. I knew about Lewis and Clark, and Pike and Frémont and Jim Bridger, but couldn't tell you a thing about the land they explored. All I knew was that it was big and beautiful and unspoiled, powerful enough to overwhelm us with its beauty, wild enough to swallow us in its vastness or bury us under its rapids, if we weren't careful. But at the same time it was at our mercy, because our carelessness could so easily burn its forests or pollute its waters or destroy the beauty that time and nature had worked for thousands of years to create.

When we got back to camp, Fox and I studied the map while Bruce went about cleaning the stove. According to the map we were just a few miles from a small town called Anson, which was a good thing since we'd be able to stock up on fresh supplies there before pushing off. It's nice to be out in the wilds, but it's also nice to have a bit of civilization handy when you need it.

And then we found ourselves being stared at. I

couldn't say for how long the four youths had been standing there, because when I first noticed them they looked like they'd been standing there for a while, and there was no telling how long they might have gone on standing and staring if we had not noticed them.

They appeared to be about our age, around seventeen or eighteen. They didn't look too friendly, but they didn't look unfriendly either. They had a kind of very frank curiosity about them; I mean, they were staring at us to the point where it was beginning to be impolite. They were wearing workpants and plaid shirts. A couple of them looked real sturdy. One of them, somehow he appeared to be the oldest, or at least the leader, had longer and shaggier hair than the others. He was the one who finally spoke up. And even then it wasn't to say much.

"Howdy," he said.

"Howdy," Fox said. He had a bright, wide smile that must have really knocked the girls over in that little Massachusetts town he came from, and he flashed it now. The shaggy one didn't smile, but still he looked more curious than unfriendly. The four youths moved in closer now, staring at everything.

"You fellas campin' out here?" one of them asked.

"That's right," Fox said. "For a day or two or three. Depending."

"On what?"

"On what we find around here. What's interesting in these parts?"

The four of them looked at each other and smiled.

"There's nothing much interesting around here," the shaggy one said.

"Oh, come now," Fox said. "You've got these beautiful mountains and the river and all sorts of natural wonders. People come from all over the world to see them."

"You'd be surprised how easily you can set sick and tired looking at natural wonders," the shaggy one said. He was pretty cool.

Two of them went and looked at our canoe, tapping it lightly with their toes, the way you kick the tires of a new car. I watched them. I don't think I trusted them. That's what comes from being a New Yorker— you have very guarded feelings about strangers, if not outright mistrust. I try to fight it, but there it is. A New Yorker takes to mistrust and suspicion like a duck takes to water.

"How far is the town from here?" I asked.

"Couple of miles," one of them said.

"In which direction?"

One of them turned around and pointed.

"A road picks up right the other side of those trees," he said.

"Where you fellows from?" the shaggy one asked.

"I'm from Massachusetts," Fox said. "My friends are from New York. How about you fellows?"

"We're all from right here," the shaggy one said.

"Interesting," Fox said. Why it was so interesting, I couldn't say. But that was Fox, always serious and polite. "Can we offer you some coffee?" he asked. There he was again, good old Foxy. Showing the real spirit of the Old West—when strangers show up, offer to break bread with them. Just like in the movies.

"No, thank you," the shaggy one said.

Just as well, I thought, since there wasn't any left.

Now I noticed two of them looking at Bruce. He had stopped working on the stove when they showed up and was standing there staring back at them. He had a calm, shrewd, knowing look on his face. He told me once that black people know when somebody doesn't like the color of their skin. It's a sixth sense, an instinct, that black people have, he said. I could see now that that instinct had picked up a few vibrations.

One of the two passed a remark quietly to his friends and they both laughed.

"Excuse me," Fox said. "But may we share in the joke?"

"What joke?" the shaggy one asked.

"Your friends here just made some remark."

Now the two stopped laughing.

"It wasn't nothin' so bad," one of them said.

"He said that you fellas must be so rich," the other one said, "that you brought along your own butler on a campin' trip."

The four all laughed.

"That's traveling real fancy," the shaggy one said.

"I think that's an insult," Fox said sharply.

"He's the same as we are," I said.

"If not better," Bruce said.

"Then maybe your friends can't be very much," the shaggy one said to him.

Oh, no, I thought. I took a quick look around. The big flashlight was handiest to me. I'd have to remember not to hit anybody too hard—I didn't want to break the flashlight.

"I think you fellows ought to move along," Fox said.

"Except that we live here," the shaggy one said. "It's *our* land here."

"Which you stole from the Indians," I said. After all, I *was* a history major.

"Oh," the shaggy one said with a smile, "they put up a pretty good fight for it."

They started to leave then, straggling off one at a time. When they had gone a little way, one of them turned around and said, "Look out for the Indians now."

They all laughed, and then they were gone.

We stood silently for a few minutes; then the tension began to ebb.

"Local yokels," Fox said.

"Harmless," I said.

"All the same," Bruce said, "we'd better not leave the camp unattended. They look like they've got loose fingers."

I really wasn't overly concerned about the four youths; they seemed to me wise guys more than anything else. All the same, I thought Bruce's warning about not leaving the camp unguarded was sensible.

After dinner we sat around writing letters to girl friends and families, to be mailed in town the next day. Then we built a fire, not because we needed one but because a fire is a nice day's-end thing when you're camping. It's very relaxing and gets you to dreaming with your eyes open. Sometimes, on chilly nights, we used the fire for warmth, and at other times to dry our clothing. But most of the time we just sat around it and stared into its leaping flames and let our thoughts run free.

Later, after the fire had burned down to a scowling little bed of bright embers, we got ready for sleep. A stiff, chill breeze had come up out of the northwest, so we decided to sleep in the tent. We inflated our air mattresses, then placed our sleeping bags on them and climbed inside.

We lay there listening to the sound of the river going by, quiet and steady.

"Tomorrow morning," Bruce said, "I'll hike into town and buy some grub."

"You might be a pioneer yet," I said. "I'll bet you'll be the first black man ever in that town."

"A little soul can't hurt anybody," Bruce said.

"Well," Fox said, "I'll be busy hammering out some of those dents in the canoe."

We'd struck some rocks here and there, putting a few creases in the canoe. These were easily pounded out.

"I'm going to collect my thoughts tomorrow," I

said. I'd been keeping a journal of the trip. It was pretty dull so far—the journal, not the trip. I was hoping to get it published when we got back, but I was going to need some grizzly bears or daredevil adventures in the rapids to spice it up.

We were all just dozing off when we heard a noise outside. At first nobody said anything; I think we were all pretending it hadn't happened. If there's one thing a city boy can't ever get used to, it's a noise in the great dark outdoors. Finally Fox said, "All right. Somebody make a guess."

"Grizzly," I said.

"Rattlesnake," Bruce said.

We listened again. We heard something again, a very slight sound.

"Maybe the canoe is sliding into the water," I said.

"Could be a mountain lion," Bruce said.

"Or those guys," Fox said.

"I'm too tired to fight," I said.

"Those kids were something else, weren't they?" Bruce said. "They say it's their land. I felt like telling them about all the places *I* own. Like the Black Sea and the Black Hills and the Black Forest."

"You got your rights out here, too, man," I said. "You could tell them you're somewhat related to the Blackfeet Indians."

"Right on," Bruce said. "And don't forget the blacksmiths that helped build the land, and the blackberries that grow on it and the blackbirds that fly over it."

"Don't forget the Black Plague," Fox said.

28

"Sorehead," Bruce said.

"Well," I said, "we've got the White Mountains and the White River and white bread."

"And the White House," Fox said.

"You got that all right," Bruce said. "Plus a lot of white elephants."

Then we got quiet again.

"I think it was a raccoon we heard," Fox said.

"I just heard a Fox," Bruce said.

"Listen," I said, getting out of my sack, "if it was a raccoon, I might as well be brave and have a look."

I crawled out of the tent and stood up. There was plenty of light. A bright moon hung just over the canyon wall, casting a soft, rippling silver light over the running water. I looked around in the moonlight. Nothing in the camp seemed to have been disturbed. I could hear the wind passing through the trees, rustling the leaves. There was perfect stillness in the moon shadows.

"Nothing," I said, crawling back inside the tent. "I had a look around."

"Gee, Steve," Bruce said, turning over in his sack. "Just think: if there had been a bear out there, you could have been a hero."

"I don't care what you say," I said, snuggling in. "We *did* hear something out there."

There was no doubt about that.

Chapter IV

The wilderness looks better in the daytime. I don't think anybody would dispute that, except maybe a few owls. During the day stray noises have an innocence and all shadows are turned to bright and friendly sunlight.

We rose early. You do that when you're camping. Every bit of daylight is precious, because usually you're moving from place to place and there's something different to see and enjoy all the time.

After breakfast we made out a list of things for Bruce to buy in town. It included items like bacon, canned goods, eggs, and fresh vegetables. Also, we asked him to pick up what newspapers he could. We didn't bring along transistors because they tend to sound noisy when nature is quietly around you, but you do get curious about what's going on in the world.

After Bruce took off for his hike to town, Fox and I busied ourselves in camp. He set to hammering out the dents in the canoe, making quite a racket. I went off a little way and found a shady spot where I was able to work quietly on my journal.

Later we made lunch, and after that I took a nap on

the grass near the river. It was a lovely sound to be lulled to sleep by. When I wakened, a few hours later, I opened my eyes to see a squirrel up in a tree, staring down at me from his branch office. I waved at him and he ran away.

When I got back to camp, Fox was sitting reading a book.

"Where's Bruce?" I asked.

"He's not back yet."

I looked at my watch. It was almost four o'clock.

"He's been gone a long time," I said.

"He's probably sightseeing. You know how he is."

Another hour passed and we began to get concerned. I was getting ready to hike into town to look for Bruce when we heard the sound of a car nearby.

"Company," I said.

A man was coming through the brush. He was kind of stocky, with a big belly, much too big a belly for a man who didn't appear to be more than thirty. He was bareheaded, wearing a khaki shirt and trousers. When he came closer we could see the tin star pinned over his shirt pocket and the pistol in the holster on his hip.

He came walking across the clearing toward us, very slowly.

"Hello, fellas," he said.

"Are you a policeman?" Fox asked.

"That's right. Deputy Sheriff Logan."

"What can we do for you?" I asked.

"Are you friends of a black fella named Bruce Price?"

"Yes. Why?"

"Well," Logan said, running his hand back through his thick black hair, "he's in some trouble now."

"Bruce?" Fox asked. "What are you talking about?"

"How well do you know him?" Logan asked.

"He's a close friend. We're all roommates in college."

"Roommates? Hey. Well." Logan grinned, nodding his head. I guess to him the idea of white and black rooming together was funny.

"Will you please tell us what's happened?" I asked.

"We have your roommate in the lock-up."

"What for?"

"Robbery."

"You must be kidding."

Logan shook his head. "Unh-unh," he said.

"But that's crazy," Fox said. "He went into town this morning to buy some supplies."

"That may be so, but he seems to have stopped along the way and broken into somebody's house."

"Bruce?" I asked. I couldn't believe it.

"That's right."

"There's some mistake, officer, I assure you," Fox said.

Logan showed a slow smile; actually it was more like he was showing us his teeth than smiling.

"We don't think so," he said.

Logan suggested we come into town with him. I don't know if it was a suggestion or an order, but

32

either way we were anxious to see Bruce. We figured we could straighten this thing out as soon as we got there. It was all so crazy—like a practical joke. Except that this was a real policeman and he was dead serious.

It wasn't a long ride in, maybe two miles. At first it was over some rough, unpaved road, then onto a smooth, blacktopped road that headed straight into town.

And then we arrived in the town of Anson. It had a small main street that ran for four blocks. It wasn't as dead or hayseed as a lot of small towns because there was some industry in the surrounding area, and on the way in we saw quite a few attractive ranch houses scattered about.

You could see which were the old, original buildings on main street and how the town had extended out from them. All of the buildings were low, some of the stores having apartments or offices over them. The lone exception was a professional building three stories high in the heart of town, which contained the offices of lawyers and doctors and dentists and real-estate and insurance people. It was called the Delume Building.

There weren't many people on the street; there seldom are in these towns during the day.

The police station was located in a detached brick building on a side street. There was a big hardware store across the street, and when we pulled up I noticed a half dozen men standing there, watching us. They were quiet.

There was a wooden sign over the door of the police station, which had "Sheriff's Office" written on it. Logan went in first, and we followed him. He closed the door behind us.

The office was one room, with bars on the windows. There was a glass case against one wall holding a half dozen rifles. On another wall was a bulletin board tacked over with "Wanted" posters, with those faces of strangers, front and profile, that you see up on post-office walls.

There was a man sitting behind the desk. He was the sheriff—he was wearing a tin star that said so. He was sort of a thin fellow, up toward fifty in years, with a tough, weathered face. He was smoking a cigar that was narrow as a pencil.

"Here they are, Sheriff," Logan said after we came in and the door was closed.

The sheriff nodded to us, looking us over with eyes that were very sharply narrowed, as if he had the sun in them. We introduced ourselves and he told us his name—Jim Beeson. Sheriff Jim Beeson.

"I wish you would clear up this situation for us, sir," Fox said. "We can't believe our friend is guilty of anything."

"Is he here?" I asked.

"He's in the back," the sheriff said. A corridor led away from the office and we could see a few cell doors back there, barred and gloomy-looking.

"Can we see him?" I asked.

34

"In a little while," the sheriff said. "I just want to ask you a few questions." He put his cigar in an ashtray now, and it lay there, the smoke curling up from it.

He wanted to know where we were from, how long we were planning to camp there, where we'd been, if we had police records. He didn't write any of it down, just sat back in his chair with his hands folded behind his head, watching us with those narrow eyes, not saying any more than he had to. Logan turned a straight-backed chair around and sat backwards on it, resting his folded arms on it. Whenever I glanced at him he had a sly little grin. I didn't like him much.

"What time did Mr. Price leave for town this morning?" Beeson asked.

"Nine o'clock," I said.

"You're sure?"

"I remember looking at my watch."

"Did you fellows have any trouble down by the river yesterday?"

"Trouble?"

"With some of our local boys."

"Four of them showed up," Fox said, "made some insulting remarks to Bruce, then left. That was the extent of it."

"Well, today," Beeson said, "they jumped him on his way into town."

"What do you mean?" I asked.

"I guess my good deputy didn't tell you about it."

35

"I didn't tell them nothing," Logan said.

"Soon after your friend left camp," Beeson said, talking in a slow, thoughtful drawl as if he were studying each word before he spoke it, "these four boys jumped him, on the dirt road. They knocked him down and mussed him up some but didn't really hurt him."

"What have you done about it?" Fox asked. "That's assault and battery. Are you going to bring them in?"

"Not unless Mr. Price prefers charges, and at the moment he's not talking much."

"Is he hurt?" I asked.

"No, no. The brawl wasn't a mean one; more mischief than anything else. He's not hurt. He's just not talking."

"Could you please tell us what he's accused of robbing?" I asked.

"Just coming to that," Beeson said. "He's accused of breaking into the home of one Mrs. Delume and making off with some of her jewelry."

"This is crazy," I said. "First you tell us he's beaten up by some of your local wise guys; then you tell us he broke into somebody's house and stole jewelry. None of this makes sense, Sheriff."

"What makes you so sure he robbed this house?" Fox asked. "What kind of proof do you have? Or do you just lock up a man because . . ." He didn't finish, letting it hang on the air.

Beeson stared at him, long and hard and critically.

Logan made a soft laughing sound, deep in his throat.

"Because what, Mr. Huntington?" Beeson asked.

"Because he's a stranger," I said, after Fox continued to let it hang.

"I see," Beeson said. "We'll get to that in a moment. I want to get back to something. You said he left your camp at nine o'clock. Where was he heading?"

"For town, to buy supplies," I said.

"He was coming straight in?"

"That's right."

"All right. From your campsite it's about a thirty-minute walk, say forty-five minutes if a fellow is taking his time. Now, Mr. Price arrived in town at about eleven thirty. That's two and a half hours."

"Well, you're forgetting something," I said. "He was beat up on the way in. That could have slowed him down, don't you think?" I guess I was sounding pretty sarcastic.

"I'm sure it could have," Beeson said. He let the sarcasm pass. He never raised his voice or changed the steady, watchful look in his face. "Now, they jumped him on the dirt road—we know about where. He was maybe fifteen or twenty minutes away from your campsite. Let's say he sat around for even thirty minutes to catch his breath. So let's say it took him forty-five minutes to walk in, and that he sat around for thirty minutes. That leaves approximately another hour and fifteen minutes of loose time, time that he can't account for. Now, on his way in he had to pass

37

the Delume house. That gives him time to enter it, steal the jewelry, hide it somewhere and finish coming into town."

"That's fantastic," I said.

"What was he doing for that hour and fifteen minutes?" Beeson asked.

"Ask him," I said.

"We did. But he's not talking."

"You had no business arresting him," I said. "Not with that kind of evidence. It's not even circumstantial."

"What made you arrest him?" Fox asked.

"Mr. Delume reported the robbery at about the time your friend appeared in town. Naturally, seeing a stranger, Mr. Logan brought him here and questioned him."

"But the robbery could have occurred last night—when we were all together," I said.

"Mr. Delume said that his mother saw the jewelry late last night, just before going to bed," Beeson said. "This morning, though she didn't look at the jewelry, she said that nothing looked disturbed. It wasn't until late in the morning that she discovered the theft. But before we could get out there, your friend showed up in town."

"But if they were home this morning," I said, "how could Bruce just walk in there and rob the place?"

"Mrs. Delume was in her garden," Beeson said, "and her son was not on the premises. They have a cook, but she's off today. So you see, we're not just shooting in the dark."

"So you nabbed Bruce," Fox said.

"Mr. Logan brought him here and searched him," Beeson said. Then he got quiet for a few moments, holding it back, because this was what he'd been building to the whole time, step by step, word by word, wanting to find out all we knew before he let it fall. "The reason we arrested your friend," he said, "is because we found one of the stolen items in his possession."

Chapter V

We just stood there thunderstruck. I'd say at least a
minute or two went by before a word was spoken.
Beeson kept his eyes fixed on us, and so did Logan,
who had a tight little smile on his lips. I guess he was
feeling like the big hero, having picked up Bruce and
having found the piece of stolen jewelry.

Frankly I didn't know what to think. All I knew for
sure was that it was all one big mistake, that there was
some explanation for it. Bruce just wasn't the type to
walk along a country road and then on the spur of the
moment take it into his head to go into somebody's
house and rob them.

Then the door opened and a man came in. He was
kind of short, about thirty-five or so, with very thin
blond hair. He was wearing a suit and tie. He seemed
sort of nervous and fidgety. When he saw Fox and me,
his mouth got very tight, as if he wouldn't talk unless
you held a match to him.

"Hello, Garvin," Beeson said. Then he looked at us.
"This is Mr. Garvin Delume," he said. "It was his
house that was robbed."

Delume shot a look at us with the corners of his
eyes.

"How's your ma, Garvin?" Logan asked.

"She's all right now," Delume said. "She's resting. It was quite a shock. Nothing like this has ever happened around here before."

"Well, you can rest easy," Logan said. "We've got the fellow locked up."

"Did you check around the house?" Beeson asked.

"Yes," Garvin Delume said. "It seems just the jewelry is missing. Some diamonds, two rings and a brooch. All very valuable. Have you recovered any more of it?"

"Just the one diamond," Beeson said.

"Mr. Delume," I said, "I can assure you that as far as Bruce Price is concerned there has to be some mistake. He's simply not a thief."

"I'm sorry," Delume said, "but I can't talk to you about it. I'll talk only to the police."

"Bruce is not a thief," Fox said.

"Then what was he doing with one of my mother's diamonds in his pocket?" Delume said. He still wasn't looking at us; he kept his eyes fixed on Beeson. He was quite nervous, his hands couldn't keep still, folding and unfolding, going in and out of his pockets. I guess he was afraid of us, afraid we might hit him over the head and take the rest of his money or something.

"We hope to find out what Mr. Price was doing with that diamond," Beeson said. He seemed very respectful of Delume. And then I remembered the building with the Delume name on it; this fellow was probably a big gun in town.

"Can we see Bruce now?" I asked.

41

"You can do that," Beeson said. "Walk back there and you'll find him."

We went into the corridor behind the office. There were four cells, two on either side. Three were empty. Bruce was sitting alone in the fourth, on the edge of a cot. He looked forlorn and lonely. The cell didn't hold much more than the cot and a toilet and a washstand. The concrete walls were whitewashed. There was a small window, with bars. Way out, behind the bars, we could see the mountains.

Bruce stood up when he saw us and came to the bars, wrapping his fingers around them.

"You know something?" he said. "Tomorrow is my birthday." He tried to smile but wasn't very successful at it.

"Bruce," Fox said, "tell us what happened."

"We're going to get you out of here," I said. "So tell us everything that happened."

His story was pretty much the same as we'd been told. He had left the campsite, gone a little way, then been jumped by the same four guys we'd seen yesterday. They'd roughed him up a little, not too badly.

"They weren't particularly mean," he said. "They didn't use their feet or anything like that. I clipped two of them. We rolled around in the dirt, and then they went away."

"Then what?"

"I sat around for a while, then dusted myself off and came into town."

"How long did you sit around?" Fox asked.

"Maybe a half hour. I was going to come back to the camp, but then I figured I might as well go on in."

He told us the rest: he had come into town, been stopped by Logan and taken to the police station. Logan searched him and found the diamond.

"But how did it get into your pocket?" I asked.

"I don't know," Bruce said. "I honestly don't know."

"Could he have planted it on you?" Fox asked.

"It's possible. Anything is possible."

"Listen," Fox said, "according to the sheriff you took an awfully long time coming in. Where were you? Why did it take so long?"

He looked at us for a second, then his eyes dropped.

"I just walked in," he said quietly. "I don't know how long it took."

"They say there's about an hour and fifteen minutes that they can't account for," I said. "They're holding that against you."

"I just walked in," he said again.

It gave me a funny feeling, the way he said it, and I think Fox must have felt the same thing, because neither of us pushed it further.

"We're going to get you out of here," Fox said. "They're not getting away with this. It's obviously a frame-up."

Bruce looked at us and smiled ruefully.

"You know," he said, "when I was a kid, about twelve years old, I was sitting in the school yard playing cards with some of my friends. The cops came in and just for a scare picked us up and put us in a cell for an hour. I was scared, but it didn't bother me too much. But to be in a jail out here, when I can see those mountains and smell that air, well, it just doesn't seem right."

"We'll get you out of here," I said.

"Even if we have to blow this place up," Fox said.

"You'd better be careful, man," Bruce said. "They have three more empty cells."

We went back to the office. Garvin Delume was gone.

"Everything okay, boys?" Beeson asked. He had the cigar in his teeth now, smoking away.

"Not really," I said.

"He tell you what he did with his time?" Logan asked.

"He says he doesn't know how that diamond got into his pocket," I said. "That's the main thing he told us."

"He told us the same," Beeson said.

"Now you didn't expect him to say he walked in and robbed that house, did you?" Logan asked.

"We'll be back," Fox said.

When we went outside we saw that the group across the street had grown to about twenty people. One loudmouthed guy was talking to them, waving his arms as he talked.

"You can see why they've got trouble in the cities,"

he was saying, "and why we've been spared out here. Why, we never had anything like this in Anson. Then one day, one of them walks into town and boom! look what we've got."

A girl, about seventeen or eighteen, looked at us, then walked in a hurry away from the crowd.

"I'm not saying we should be bigots," the loudmouth was saying. "I'm as fair about these things as the next man. All I'm saying is that people should stay where they belong and not bring their brand of trouble into somebody else's backyard."

"That'll do if you please, Mr. Ackroy."

We turned around. It was Sheriff Beeson, standing behind us in the doorway of the police station. The loudmouth shut up. Everybody looked across the street at Beeson, and at us, too, I guess. I swear, it was a scene out of a Western movie, where the sheriff decides to speak out against a mob for the underdog. It wasn't a lynch mob, of course, but I still didn't like the look of them.

The loudmouth—Ackroy—looked at Beeson and stopped talking. The people started to drift away. I hadn't noticed that many people around when we came into town, but just let somebody start talking trouble and he'll draw a crowd in the middle of a desert.

Beeson stood there and watched them all go, Ackroy included.

"You fellows want a ride back to your site?" Beeson asked.

"No thanks," I said. "We'll hike it."

As we walked out of town there were people here and there watching us, from the sidewalks, from behind the windows of the restaurants. When you're in a strange town and people look at you like that, it makes you feel like a criminal.

Chapter VI

I can tell you it was a long, slow walk back to the river. We had a lot to sort out in our minds: noises in the night, those four guys roughing up Bruce, the robbery, Bruce being arrested—and that one big thing which weighed so heavily: the diamond's being found in Bruce's pocket.

We barely noticed the scenery now as we walked, though it was as wild and beautiful as ever. We passed some hilly woodland and then broad fields all bright and alive with flowers blowing in the breeze. But it hardly caught our eye at all.

"Maybe we ought to get him a lawyer," I said.

"Who? Where?" Fox asked. "Put his fate in the hands of one of these yokels and they'll railroad him for sure. You heard that guy talking. If we get him a lawyer, it'll be somebody from New York."

"Well, we should do something about it."

"It's all so wrong," Fox said thoughtfully. "It just smells so fishy."

"That guy Logan could well have planted the stone on Bruce."

"But why?"

"Maybe he's in with whoever really took the stuff. If they're successful in pinning it on Bruce, then they're clear. If we can find out his movements this morning, we might be on to something."

"But how?" Fox asked.

"Maybe Beeson can find out. He impressed me as being a pretty straight guy."

"Ask one cop to investigate another? You're naïve, boy."

"It happens," I said.

"Not in a town this size."

I looked out at the flowers now, and the mountains beyond. It looked like a calendar picture, all so bright and beautiful, thriving under a perfectly blue, cloudless sky.

We passed some homes and then, farther along, we came to a driveway cutting in off of the road. The letter box at the entrance said "Delume." We stopped and looked into the driveway. The house was a few hundred feet in, behind some trees. It looked pretty fancy.

"That old lady should have kept her jewels in a bank vault," I said.

"I tell you, whoever took them knew the layout pretty well," Fox said. "He would have to. The old lady was in the garden, her creepy son was out of the house and the cook was off. It *had* to be a local person."

We started walking again. We were both pretty glum and stayed quiet for a time. As we neared the camp, Fox said, "Bruce was pretty uptight, wasn't he?"

"Wouldn't *you* be?"

"You know what struck me as odd?"

"What?" I asked.

"He seemed kind of vague about the missing time. Now that's a big chunk of time--an hour and fifteen minutes. He seemed to clam up when we asked him about it, didn't he?"

"So what?"

"So where was he, what was he doing?"

"Fox—"

"Look," he said, "we have to be open-minded about this. We have to look at the facts coldly, because that's how Beeson is looking at them. If we want to know what he's thinking, we have to do that."

"Are you saying—"

"I'm not saying anything except what I think Beeson is thinking," Fox said. "He's quite obviously thinking that the reason Bruce has no explanation for the missing time—or at least won't give one—is because during that time Bruce broke into the house, stole the jewelry and then buried it, all except for the one piece which they found in his pocket, which he probably overlooked and didn't know he was carrying. That's what Beeson thinks."

"But is that what you think?" I asked.

"Steve, right at this moment, that's not what I think. And anyway, what I think is not important. Let's open the discussion to every possibility. Before you put me on the hot seat, let's hear *your* explanation for the missing hour and fifteen minutes."

I didn't have any.

"Now put yourself in Bruce's place," Fox said. "You're walking along minding your own business and four clowns jump you for no good reason other than your skin is black. He must have been pretty sore. Remember, he's had a lifetime of this nonsense. It can boil up on you after a while."

"So you're saying that the drubbing he took so angered him that he lost his head and walked into the first house he saw and robbed it, just to get even."

"People have been known to do stranger things. When a person finally decides to retaliate, he strikes out at the first available target. He could have come to that driveway, his blood still boiling, looked in, saw the house and decided to do some mischief. Let's say the door is open; he spots the old lady in the garden, no one else seems to be around, so he walks inside . . ."

"In his frame of mind it could have been possible," I said.

"Maybe he takes the jewelry not to really have it but just to get even for all the abuse he's had to take all his life. Let's say he even throws the stuff away later, because he's not really a criminal and doesn't actually want it, except for the one piece that he overlooks."

We walked quietly for a while. Then I suddenly stopped.

"Fox," I said. "Do you realize what we're doing? We're saying he's guilty. Oh, sure, we're saying he had good reason, we're giving him every excuse and explanation—but we're still saying he did it. And what's more, what's worse—why are we saying it? Because he's black. We're saying that because a black man has been wronged he immediately turns to crime in order to get even. We're using the same point of departure that bigots do."

Fox put his hand up to his cheek. "My God," he said softly. "We are, aren't we?"

"And if *we* think that, then what chance does Bruce have?"

"Listen, I never said he was guilty," Fox said quickly. "All I was doing was speculating."

"That was pretty strong speculation."

"You went along with it, buddy."

"I was being polite," I said.

"Well, I don't care what I said. I don't believe he did it. And I resent myself for even having breathed the merest notion of it."

Fox was sore at himself. It was almost funny. What can a fellow do when he's sore at himself? He just pressed his lips in and looked around in great confusion, as if looking for someplace where he could do himself some harm. Suddenly he shot out his hand.

"Bruce is not guilty," he said, as if he were the head of a jury or something. "Shake on it?"

We shook on it.

Then we walked on. As we got close to the camp, to where the dirt road ran out, we saw a car parked there. When we got to the camp, we saw we had company.

51

Chapter VII

She was standing near the tent, looking out toward the river. She was wearing blue jeans and a checked shirt. Her hair was long and free-falling, the color of honey. When she turned around and saw us, I realized this was the girl we had seen in town, who had been part of the crowd listening to the loudmouth. She was a good-looking girl, too, though right now that lovely face of hers was wearing a very determined look.

When she saw us, she began walking toward us through the late-afternoon shadows.

"Are you or are you not going to try and help your friend?" she asked.

The question, shot out just like that, took us by surprise, and for a few seconds we didn't say anything, just stood there staring at this very lovely girl.

"He's in serious trouble you know," she said.

"We know that of course," Fox said. He could get a little stuffy when somebody told him something he already knew.

"And of course we're going to try and help him," I said.

Now she smiled, briefly.

"Good," she said. "We'll work together. Great."

Then she started talking. She talked quickly, like

someone who's been storing her words and becomes terrifically excited at the prospect of finally having a chance to release them. She knew everything that happened, she said. In a town as small as Anson, what flew were not rumors but whole stories. She said that by yesterday afternoon everybody in town knew that we were camping by the river, that one of us was black, that we were planning on staying a few days. Then she heard what happened today.

"I don't believe a word of any of it," she said. "Your friend is being made a scapegoat." There seemed no doubt in her mind of it.

"That's exactly what we think," Fox said. He was amazing; not five minutes ago he had me half convinced Bruce was guilty.

"I won't say that people in this town are prejudiced," she said. "It's just that they're ignorant about things and people they don't know anything about."

"We know," I said. "We heard that guy talking in town."

She paused for a moment.

"I've been hearing him talk all my life," she said. "He's my father."

Oh.

"But never mind that," she said. "He's the least of it. I'm not going to apologize for him; he has his opinions and I have mine."

Her name was Wilma Ackroy—she was called Wilcie by everybody—and she was a real ball of fire, besides being good-looking in a nice, fresh, outdoors sort of way. She was a journalism major at a Midwestern college, home for the summer now and getting experience working part-time on the local paper. She was absolutely convinced that Bruce was innocent, was angry about what was happening and was determined to do something about it. She was as excited and energetic as somebody about to launch a crusade.

"Do you want to help him?" she asked.

"Of course," Fox said.

"Well, there's nothing you can do for him standing around here," she said.

She told us that Beeson was planning to talk to the four youths who had jumped Bruce, and that perhaps we ought to see what we could find out from them. So we got into her car and headed back to town.

The sun was beginning to set now, bathing the sky in wild, rosy colors. The shadows were lengthening. Here and there the river threw out a flash of sunset color.

When we reached the police station, we found the four youths there, getting a stern lecture from Beeson. We came in in time to hear him saying that they were getting away lucky, that Bruce had decided not to press charges, that if he wanted to, he could charge them with assault and battery and either sue them or have them sent to jail. He laid it on pretty thick; I could see he was quite sore at them and wanted to scare them as badly as he could.

The four of them looked sheepish when they saw us. Even the one with the shaggy hair, who had been the leader, seemed embarrassed and avoided looking at us.

"You think you're big heroes," Beeson said, "piling on one man like that. I'd like to see any of you try it by yourselves. Any of you want to go back there and get into that cell with him alone?"

There were no takers, just a lot of uncomfortable shuffling of feet and lowering of eyes. Then he told them to take off, with the warning that from now on he was going to keep a sharp eye on them, that if he so much as caught one of them spitting on the sidewalk, he'd run the guy in. Then they left.

"They're not bad kids, really," Beeson said. "Mischievous more than anything else."

"Some mischief," Fox said. "Where I come from, they'd be in plenty trouble for what they did."

"Well, Mr. Huntington," Beeson said, "you're not where you come from now; you're where you're at. I guess where you come from you have so much of this you know better how to handle it than we do."

"What did you get out of them, Jim?" Wilcie asked.

"I see you've taken on the case," Beeson said, grinning at her.

"I'm a newspaperwoman, remember," she said.

"Yes," he said. "And as an elected official I suppose I should cooperate with the press."

"Especially since you're up for reelection this November," she said. This girl didn't fool around.

"Haven't said yet if I'm running again," he said.

"Well, I hope you do run. You're an excellent sheriff, in my opinion."

"All right," he said, sitting down at his desk. "I'll tell you what I can. They admitted it readily enough. Said they did it just for fun, that they really didn't have anything against Price. They just wanted to break the monotony. A prank. Not a very nice one, but a prank all the same."

"Sheriff," I said, "suppose it had been me or Fox walking on that road. What would have happened?"

"I don't know. But I did get the impression it was Bruce Price they were after."

"How did they know, I wonder, that Bruce would be the one going to town?"

"That's a good question, Mr. Miller," Beeson said.

"Did you ask it?" Wilcie asked.

"I did," the sheriff said. "The answer was that they decided to take the chance."

"Do you mean to say," Fox said, "that just on an off-chance they got up early and went out there and hid in the bushes, hoping Bruce would come along?"

"It sounds peculiar, but that's what they did. Now, these boys don't have much to do. None of them are working at the moment; they don't have any money, not that there's much for them to spend it on around here even if they did. So sitting out there in the bushes hoping your friend might pass is quite an activity for them."

"Have you spoken to Bruce again?" I asked.

"I had a talk with him after you left. Just the two of us. He didn't tell me any more than he had before. Still doesn't know how that diamond jumped into his pocket and won't say why it took him so long to get into town. Now, I want to be fair, sir, but I'm going to have to charge him pretty soon. A district attorney is going to come here from the county seat in a day or two. If you really want to help your friend, I suggest you find him a lawyer, instead of charging off making a private investigation."

"What makes you think we're going to investigate anything?" I asked.

"I know this young lady here," he said and smiled.

"Sheriff," I said, "can I ask you a delicate question?" I had to. I knew it was crazy, but I had to.

"You can *ask* anything," he said.

"Is there the slightest possibility that your deputy, while in the act of searching Bruce, could have planted the diamond on him?"

He fixed me with a very hard stare.

"I'd call that an *in*delicate question, Mr. Miller," he said. "I'll answer you by saying that George Logan has worked with me for four years, and I have no reason to suspect him of being capable of doing anything dishonest. Now I wish you'd drop that line of thinking from your mind."

I didn't quite drop it, although I did move it aside a bit.

Then we went back and spoke to Bruce again, introducing him to Wilcie. She promised faithfully that we would prove his innocence, that we wouldn't sleep until we did, and things like that. It cheered him up some, but not much. He was still pretty glum. It was

57

dark in there now. There was no light in the cell, and the corridor light was not yet turned on. So he seemed really sealed up in that cell.

"You fellows are going to stick around, aren't you?" he asked.

"Of course," Fox said.

"Can we bring you anything?" I asked.

Bruce wrapped his fingers around the bars of the cell door.

"The key," he said.

Chapter VIII

"He's innocent," Wilcie said as we walked along the street. "I can tell. All my instincts tell me."

"But what about the diamond?" I asked. "And the missing hour and fifteen minutes?"

"We're going to find out about those things," she said.

I said to Fox, "Do you want to tell Wilcie about what you were speculating before?"

He gave me a real dirty look.

"What was that?" she asked.

"Nothing, it's nothing," he said in a hurry.

I was glad there were no laws against kidding Fox. It would have made life painfully dull.

It was getting dark now. Anson wasn't the liveliest place at night. There was a movie theater that opened at seven o'clock, an ice-cream parlor, a restaurant and a bar. Otherwise Main Street had rolled over and gone to sleep for the night.

We were heading for the restaurant to have coffee when Mr. Ackroy came out of the bar. He was a big, beefy man with a red face. He looked as if he got excited easily and often.

"Where are you going, Wilcie?" he asked, giving Fox and me a quick, disapproving glance.

"I'm covering a story," she said.

He made a face. You could see it wasn't easy for him having a daughter who fancied herself a hotshot reporter.

"Well, it's getting dark," Ackroy said, pulling his pants up over his big belly.

"Most news is made at night," she said.

Now he looked square at me.

"Are you fellows leaving town?" he asked.

"Not until we can take our friend with us," I said.

"That means you'll be around for a long time, from what I hear," he said.

"Don't be so sure," I said. "We've got some surprises up our sleeves."

"Like what?" he asked.

"A surprise isn't a surprise until it's sprung at the unexpected moment," I said. "This isn't the moment." I really didn't know what I was talking about, but I thought it might be good strategy to drop a few hints, especially to a bigmouth like this fellow. If there was a guilty party around town, he'd hear about it, and it might just make him nervous enough to make a few slips. I've read a few detective novels in my time.

"What makes you want to travel around with a colored?" he asked.

"He's our friend," I said.

"But you see he can get you into trouble."

"And anyway, Father," Wilcie said, "they're not called colored anymore; they're called blacks."

Ackroy laughed.

"You can't change the look of midnight by changing its name," he said.

"I heard you say before, sir," Fox said, "that you weren't a bigot."

"That's right," Ackroy said.

"What do you have against bigots?" Fox asked.

Ackroy gave him a suspicious look. Wilcie spoke up.

"My father knows that bigots are ignorant and dangerous," she said.

Now Ackroy looked at her. He was getting sore. His mouth tightened for a moment.

"I want you to be getting home soon," he said. He shot us a quick, definitely hostile look, then went back into the bar, hoisting his pants up over his belly again.

Wilcie looked at us. "We fight all the time," she said. "We have different points of view on everything. But I will say he's generous. When I went off to college, he bought me the car, and he's always sending me money for new clothes and things. But he does have his prejudices. I guess he was just brought up differently, that's all. We argue all the time, but . . ."

"He's still your father," I said.

She nodded, smiling.

"What does he do?" Fox asked as we walked again.

"He's the town barber."

"That's terrible," I said.

"Why?"

"It means that every few weeks he talks to every man in town."

She laughed. "But not everybody listens to him," she said. "Don't judge us all by my poor, misguided father."

We went into the restaurant and took a back table. It was a quiet place. There were a few people having dinner. It seemed to me they lowered their conversations when we walked in. I guess we were scandalous characters in town. At least *they* thought so anyway.

We ordered coffee and hamburgers.

"Tell us about Delume," Fox said after our food had been brought.

"Richest people in town," Wilcie said. "The father went into real estate years ago, and he happened to own the land that the factories wanted to build on and the land where the new post office was built. He was lucky. Right from the beginning. He had a partner who died early, and since the partner had no heirs, old man Delume took over the whole business. But the old man's luck ran out and he died, about ten years ago. The son, Garvin, runs the business now. He lives in that big house with his mother. She's an old lady now and we seldom see her in town."

"Garvin seems like a creep," I said.

"That's the word," Wilcie said. "But he's a rich creep. All the girls of his day were after him, because he was rich. But he never married. I think the old lady kept her thumbs on him. They say she controls the purse strings."

"What does he do with himself when he's not running the business?" I asked.

"He paints. He's got a little studio out behind the

house. Once a year he has a show. He lays his canvases out all over the backyard and everybody comes and says how great they are."

"Are they?"

"They're awful," she said. "But what can you tell the richest man in town? And anyway, he's not a bad sort. I feel kind of sorry for him. With all the money and the big house and everything, he seems to have missed the boat somehow."

"The old lady must be a terror," Fox said.

"I hardly know her. They say she's still mourning her husband, that there's one room in the house fixed up like sort of a shrine to him, with his pictures and belongings and everything. It's morbid. Sometimes I'm glad I was born poor."

"Fox is very rich, but he's happy," I said.

"I'm not so rich," Fox said. Rich people can sometimes be sensitive about it.

"Come off it," I said. "Your father's a big corporation lawyer. He drags home seventy-five thou a year. You said so yourself."

"All right," he said. "So what? He works hard. There's nothing wrong with it."

"Except that he robs from the poor."

Wilcie laughed.

"Steven," Fox said, "sometimes you're crude."

"All I said is that you're rich and you're happy. Aren't you happy?"

"Reasonably," he said.

"You're the only person I know who sings in his sleep."

He looked at Wilcie and shook his head.

"I put up with this all the time," he said. "From both of them. The reason I brought them out here was to lose them."

"Well, you've lost Bruce," I said.

"That's right," Wilcie said. "Bruce."

That brought us back to home plate again. We finished the meal without saying much. I guess we all felt a bit guilty about the kidding around, what with Bruce sitting in that dark little cell in the police station on the side street in this small town that nobody ever heard of, tucked away in the mountains.

When we left the restaurant we saw three of the four youths who'd jumped Bruce. They were standing on the sidewalk outside of the ice-cream parlor. Rock music was coming from inside the place, but they weren't moving to it the way kids sometimes do. They were just standing there, kind of moody.

"Let's give it a try," Wilcie said as we headed for them.

They looked away as we approached, hoping we'd pass them by, I guess. But we weren't passing them by.

"Hello, boys," Wilcie said.

None of them said anything. There were three of them; the one that was missing was the shaggy one.

"How would you like to get your names in the paper?" Wilcie asked.

"Unh-unh," one said. "We just want to forget about the whole thing."

"I don't blame you," she said. "It would look pretty crummy for you, a story in the paper about how the four of you jumped one lone guy."

They didn't say anything. They just stood there looking around, down at the ground, into the ice-cream parlor, off into the night—anywhere but at us.

"Whose idea was it?" Wilcie asked.

Now one of them looked straight at her. He seemed eager to tell.

"Walt Pike's," he said. The others agreed. Walt Pike was the absent one, the shaggy one. And I don't think they were throwing it on him just because he wasn't there; he had seemed the natural leader of them anyway, the strongest, the coolest. He seemed the kind of guy capable of talking three others into doing something they might never have thought of doing by themselves.

"Why did he want to do it?" she asked.

"Just for the fun," one said. "He said the black guy had wised off when we were at the river the day before and that we should jump him, just for the fun."

"What do you mean, 'day before'?" I asked. "When did you decide to do it?"

"This morning."

"You mean Walt called you all and said let's jump the black guy? That must have been pretty early."

"About seven thirty," one of the boys said.

"What made you all want to go at that hour?" I asked.

They shrugged, three sets of shoulders, all shrugging

together in response to a question they probably had never bothered to ask themselves.

"Walt said let's do it," one said, offering the only explanation they had.

"How did you know it would be the black guy walking on the road this morning?" Fox asked.

More shrugging shoulders. They didn't know. All they knew was that Walt had suggested they get the black guy.

"But Walt seemed to know," Wilcie said.

"All he said was let's get the black guy," one of the boys said.

"Suppose it had been one of us walking there?" I asked, referring to Fox and myself.

"I don't know," one of the boys said. They were starting to get annoyed now. "Look," he said, "the black guy went and robbed the house, didn't he? So why should we feel so bad about messing him up?"

We didn't say anything to that; there was no point. They, like just about everybody else in town, I guess, had decided that Bruce was guilty.

We walked on, along the quiet, nighttime sidewalks of Anson.

"Now what?" Fox asked.

"I think we ought to pay a visit to Walter Pike," Wilcie said.

Chapter IX

Walt Pike lived with his parents and older sister in a wooden frame house about a mile outside of town.

"What makes you think he'll tell you anything?" Fox asked Wilcie as we drove out there.

"I know him fairly well," she said. "He actually is a rather intelligent and sensitive person. His problem is he's not doing anything and has too much time on his hands."

When we got to the house, Fox and I waited outside in the car while Wilcie went in.

"So?" I said.

"So what?" he said.

"So nothing."

It was as quiet as stones out there. There were just a few houses scattered about, standing behind trees. Way out, you could just barely see the mountain line against the dark sky.

"We ought to just get him a lawyer and stop this running around," Fox said.

"Maybe she can come up with something," I said. "After all, she knows everybody around here. And she does work for the newspaper."

"That doesn't mean anything," he said. He was falling into a cranky mood now, I could tell. "We're just wasting time, letting Bruce sit in jail while we run around playing private detective."

"I've got a feeling we're going to hook into something."

"You see too many movies, Steve," he said. "That sort of thing doesn't happen in real life—people like us going out and solving the crime."

"Sure it does."

"Where? When?"

"I see it in the movies all the time," I said.

He clammed up, sitting there with his hands in his pockets, his brooding eyes staring through the windshield at the night. And I can tell you that when night comes in that part of the country, it comes with a fullness, round and deep and complete, muffling all sound and hiding all things under a great, dead weight of darkness. All you can see are those stars up there, by the billions, great clouds of them, like silver dust.

About ten minutes after she had gone in, Wilcie came out of the house, alone. She got back into the car.

"He wasn't home," she said. "But I talked to his sister. She seemed to feel something was the matter. She said Walt was particularly moody all day, like something was bothering him."

"But where is he?" I asked.

"He went up to the cabin for the night."

"What's that?"

"Last summer Walt and some of his friends built this cabin up in the mountains. They go up there once in a

while and spend the night, just to have an adventure."
She looked at us. "The boys who live out here have
the same fantasies as they do where you come from."

"Where is this place?" Fox asked.

"It isn't far," Wilcie said. "How about going there
now and talking to him?"

"Now?" Fox asked. "At night?"

"There'll be a moon coming up soon. That'll give us
enough light. And anyway, the cabin isn't in such a
remote place."

"Let's go," I said.

We followed the road out for about five miles, to a
very lonely area where there were no houses. Wilcie
began to slow down. She said there was a trail along
here that started at the side of the road and wound up
into the mountain and led to the cabin.

"What made him take off tonight?" I asked as we
rode very slowly, looking for the trail, the headlights
gliding off the roadside rocks and shrubbery. The land
on one side of the road was fairly level, on the other
it swelled and built up into the night.

"His sister doesn't know," Wilcie said. "She said he
was sitting around most of the day just staring into
space, and then when he came back from town suddenly packed his knapsack and said he was going up
to the cabin. She said that in itself wasn't unusual, but
the fact that he wanted to go alone made it seem
peculiar, that he must really be bothered by something."

Then she spotted the trail. How she did, I don't

know, since it didn't look like anything to me—just a slight break in the bushes. She pulled over to the side of the road and we all got out.

"Aren't you going to lock the car?" I asked.

"This isn't New York City," she said, laughing.

"Oh, no?" I said. "It seems to me you've got a jewel thief on the loose around here. That at least qualifies you to be a suburb."

Wilcie went first. The moon had barely come up, shedding a thin, pale light. She said it was plenty. She must have had cat eyes; I could hardly see a thing.

It wasn't a bad climb, however. The trail was winding, but it widened farther up and was pretty clear, except for occasional rocks underfoot. Once we had to stop to catch our breaths. Standing up there in the clear, cool, moon-tipped air, we were able to catch a view of Anson spread out a few miles away. There was just a scattering of lights to tell you that a town was there. The mountains were dead still: there wasn't even a breeze. But they had that night feeling again, of a deep, menacing presence.

"Any bears up here?" I asked. I whispered it. You always whisper when you ask a question like that in a place like that. Wilcie smiled.

"Oh, yes," she said. She sounded almost cheerful about it.

"What do we do if we see one?"

"That depends. If you startle him, you won't have to do anything—he'll do it all."

70

Then we started climbing again. Soon the trail began to level off somewhat, and then we saw the cabin. It stood off by itself in a little clearing, shaped out by the moonlight. A weaving red light showed in the window.

"He's got a fire going," Wilcie said.

"What do we do?" Fox asked. "Just walk in on him?"

"We didn't come all this way just to look at his cabin," I said.

"Of course we walk in on him," Wilcie said.

"Sure," I said. "Take advantage of his Western hospitality."

"Some hospitality he's shown," Fox said.

We went toward the cabin. The rosy red light was moving in the window and looked kind of inviting—from where we were standing out there in the dark.

The cabin wasn't very large and—as far as I could tell—didn't appear to have been put together too skillfully. It was sort of squared off, about ten by ten, room enough for a few guys to sit and roast hamburgers and bed down in sleeping bags.

Wilcie tapped on the door. Standing out there in the wilderness knocking on somebody's door seemed kind of strange. What was even stranger was that there was no answer. Either he wasn't answering or else he had gone to a neighbor to borrow a cup of sugar.

"Walt," Wilcie called out.

No answer.

"Maybe he doesn't want company," Fox said.

"Well," she said, putting her hand on the latch, "he's getting some."

She opened the door and we followed her inside. There wasn't much to see. The fire was going big and lusty in the fireplace, popping and crackling and snorting; a good, well-laid, well-made fire. There was a table in the middle of the plank floor and a few chairs around it. A knapsack lay on the table and a bedroll on one of the chairs. Over the fireplace was a wooden shelf holding some canned goods. That was about it. There was no Walt Pike . . . even though that was his fire and his knapsack and his bedroll.

We went to the fire, and Fox and I crouched and held out our hands. The heat rose and flattened against our outstretched palms.

"This is very strange," Wilcie said.

"There isn't another place in the area, is there?" I asked.

"No," she said.

"Then he's got to be around somewhere," Fox said.

He was. When we stood up and turned around, we saw him standing in the doorway. With a rifle in his hands.

Chapter X

So there was Walt Pike, in his rough clothing and shaggy hair; the fellow who had been so menacing yesterday at the campsite and who this morning with his friends had jumped Bruce. There he was now, holding a rifle in his hands and looking none too friendly.

"I could shoot you all," he said. "This is private property."

The moment strung out, the only sound the fire burning at our backs, crackling quietly. Then Wilcie spoke out.

"Oh, Walt," she said in an annoyed way, "put that rifle down and come in. We want to talk to you."

He did just that, too. He closed the door behind him, stood the rifle against the wall and walked in and took a chair. He sat forward at the table, resting on his arms.

"I heard you coming up the trail," he said. "I didn't know who you were, so I took my rifle and went out."

"What are you doing here?" Wilcie asked. "Why did you come up here tonight?"

He looked at her, no real expression in his face, though I think there was some interest in his eyes, the way he fixed her for a moment.

"It's my cabin," he said. "Mine and the boys'. Any of us can come up here anytime we want." Now he shifted a look to Fox and me. "Outsiders ain't welcome though."

"Stop trying to be such a tough guy," Wilcie said. "I know you for a long time, remember."

"So what?" he asked.

"So I want you to remember that we've been friends all our lives."

"I know that. I've known you exactly as long as you've known me," he said.

"Your conscience is bothering you, isn't it, Walt? You're feeling guilty about something."

"What makes you say?"

"She knows you all your life, remember," Fox said.

I gave him a look that told him to stay out of it.

"What are you going around with them for?" Walt asked her.

I thought I detected a wisp of jealousy there. Fox felt it too, from the way he threw me a quick glance.

"Their friend is in trouble and I'm trying to help them," she said.

"The black guy robbed the house. It's nobody's fault but his own."

"Why did you and your friends beat him up this morning?" Wilcie asked.

"We didn't beat him up," Walt said. "We just rolled him around a bit. Nobody got hurt."

"But why did you do it?"

"Look, I went through all this with the sheriff."

"Whose idea was it?" she asked.

He gave her a strange, sharp look.

"Everybody's," he said.

"That's not true," Wilcie said. "I spoke to your friends. They said it was *your* idea, that you called them up early this morning and suggested it."

"Well, they agreed to go."

"That's because you asked them. If one of *them* had asked you to go along with such a thing, you would have said no."

"What's that supposed to mean?"

"It means that they all do what you say. You're the leader of that little gang and if you told them to jump off a cliff, they would."

"They're my friends," he said.

"They're a bunch of brainless followers. But that's all right, too—if you want friends like that. But if they follow you around like a bunch of puppies, then you're responsible for them."

"Bull," he said. "They're responsible for themselves. I'm not their lord and master."

"But in a way you are. And if you've led them into a pack of trouble, then you have a heavier burden of guilt. And you know it."

"What are you talking about?"

"You know what I'm talking about. There's more to this whole business than has come out just yet."

He wet his underlip with his tongue, staring thoughtfully at Wilcie. Then he looked into the fire for a moment. It was starting to burn down now. The cabin was getting chillier.

"Walter," she said quietly. "There's a fellow sitting

in jail right now for something he probably didn't do. Is there any way you can help him?"

He got up now and fed the fire, throwing in some more kindling, resetting the burning logs with the poker. He stoked it just fine, with a few quick touches, and got it burning strong again.

"They say he robbed the house," he said, his back to us.

"But how do they know?"

He shrugged, his shoulders rising and falling in his corduroy jacket.

"Sheriff says it," he said.

"Do you believe it?"

He moved his head slowly to one side and looked as though he was going to say something, but he didn't. He continued to kneel there, fussing with the fire, even though it was going fine now.

"He'll get a fair trial here," he said finally. "Even if your friends here don't think so."

"But why should he stand trial for something he didn't do?"

"Ask the sheriff, don't ask me."

Now he stood, faced the fire a few moments longer, then turned. He looked at me, then Fox, then back to Wilcie, then back to me.

"I'm sorry we roughed up your friend," he said.

He sat down at the table then, opened his knapsack and took out a half loaf of unsliced rye bread and some cheese wrapped in waxed paper and a small thermos.

"We're going now, Walt," Wilcie said.

"Suit yourself," he said, not looking up.

We left the cabin, closing the door behind us. It was odd, but I felt kind of sorry for him sitting there alone in the quiet cabin up in the dark, lonely mountains. Something certainly was bothering him, and he was going to have to think it out all by his lonesome.

We went back down the trail by the light of the moon, not saying much. Fox tripped once and went tumbling into the bushes and we had to haul him out. Nothing was hurt, though, but his dignity. When we got back to the car we stood there.

"Well," Fox said, "that was a wild-goose chase."

"Do you think so?" Wilcie said.

"We didn't get anything out of him, did we? We're right back where we started."

Wilcie was watching him with a look almost of amusement, almost as if she were laughing at him. I think Fox's spill had made him a bit cranky.

"We got everything out of him, Fox," Wilcie said.

I couldn't help staring at her. I had the silliest feeling, as though I were falling in love or something like that. I felt as though I had been standing on my head for the last half hour. It was so nice and detaching a feeling that I barely heard what she said. But I got myself caught up in a hurry.

"What did you say?" I asked.

"I said we got everything out of him—everything he could tell us, anyway, up to a point."

"What are you talking about?" Fox asked.

"I know how that diamond got into Bruce's pocket."

"How?" Fox asked.

"Walt put it there."

"Wha-a-t?" Fox said. "I didn't hear him say that."

"It's not what he said, it's what he didn't say."

"Explain," Fox said folding his arms.

"I asked him how they knew Bruce robbed the house. Then I asked him why Bruce should stand trial for something he didn't do. Neither time did he mention the diamond in Bruce's pocket."

"But—" Fox said.

"What were you thinking when I asked him how they knew Bruce robbed the house?"

"Well," Fox said, scratching his head now, "I *was* wondering why he didn't mention the diamond. It *did* seem the obvious thing to say."

"Exactly. Because *he* put it there, and now it's on his conscience."

"I got it right away," I said. "I'm surprised you didn't see it, Fox."

"Nonsense you got it right away," he said. "You didn't see it any more than I did."

"Of course I did," I said, giving him the needle. "It was obvious."

"Then why didn't he come right out and admit it?" Fox asked Wilcie, which was a dumb question.

"Would you have expected him to?" she asked. "He told us all he could without coming right out with it. He told us more when he apologized for roughing up Bruce. That was very unlike him. He was apologizing for more than just some roughhouse."

78

"Then you're saying," Fox said, "that Walt and his friends robbed the house, waylaid Bruce, planted the diamond on him and . . ."

Wilcie had begun shaking her head almost as soon as he started talking. He was wrong again. I had never seen Fox so wrong so often.

"No?" he asked. He was getting confused now.

"Those boys would never do that, would never have robbed the house. In fact, I think Walt was the only one who knew about the diamond. If they had all been in on it, he wouldn't have had to call them the way he did. It would have been planned differently."

"Then what you're saying," I said, "is that somebody stole the jewelry and hired Walt to plant one piece on Bruce, to frame him."

"Right," Wilcie said.

"But who?"

"That we don't know—yet."

"It sounds possible," Fox said.

"Maybe we ought to go back up there and talk to him some more," I said.

"No," she said. "I know him. He's told us all he's going to. He's leaving it to us to figure out the rest."

"You mean he wants it all to come out?" I asked.

"Of course," she said. "His conscience is hurting him so badly he wants the truth to come out."

"Freshman psychology," Fox said. "You've stuffed your head with nonsense."

"I think she's doing just fine," I said.

I felt like kissing her. I would have, too, if Fox hadn't been there.

"Shouldn't we tell all this—for whatever it's worth—to Sheriff Beeson?" Fox asked.

"No," she said. "He would scoff, just like you did. He wouldn't say 'freshman psychology' either; he'd use a stronger word. Remember, he has to deal in facts."

"He's not brilliant like we are, Foxy," I said.

"I don't know what you're trumpeting about," he said. "All you did was stand there and let Wilcie work it out."

"I was sending thought waves to her through the air," I said.

She looked at me and smiled. She loved me, I could tell. That mountain air was doing wonders.

"Wilcie," I said, "will you marry me tomorrow?"

"I'd love to," she said. "But I have a boyfriend back at school. We're getting engaged in September."

"Oh," I said. "Then maybe the day after."

She didn't say yes, but she didn't say no either.

We got back into the car and headed for the camp-site. Wilcie dropped us off where the paved road ended because Fox and I decided we'd walk the stretch of dirt road back to the camp. It was a sweet, cool evening, good for walking. She said she'd see us in the morning after breakfast.

"You fellows get a good night's sleep," she said as she started to drive off. "We're going to be very busy tomorrow."

We began walking, two lone, quiet shadows under the great, star-sprawling sky.

"Who do you think did it, Steve?" Fox asked.

I thought about it for a while, then said, "I still support your original theory. I think Bruce did it."

He sighed, then said, "I'm out here alone in the wilderness with an imbecile."

We didn't say much as we approached the camp, and that's probably what helped cause what happened next. I don't think we made a sound as we came through the brush, or else whatever sounds we did make were covered by the noise of the river. Also, the moon had slipped behind a cloud bank and there was virtually no light.

I think we saw it at precisely the same instant—the shadow dart as we entered the campsite. We both went for it, not thinking that it might have been a bear or a mountain lion or something like that. Instinctively, we ran at the shadowy figure. Fox got there first, and the next thing I knew I was hearing the sound of a well-thrown fist landing and Fox staggering back and crashing into me. I pushed him aside and leaped toward the person, clawing at him with my hands.

"I got you," I said breathlessly.

But I didn't have him for long. He twisted around and fired two pumping fists into my middle, knocking the breath out of me for a moment. I didn't go down, but fell back, clasping my stomach, gasping. I heard Fox grappling with the guy again, and they must have been swinging around in a wild wrestle because the next thing I knew, both of them were crashing against me and I did go down.

There was an impossible tangling of bodies in the

dark and I couldn't tell who was who. I swung out at the nearest person and landed a good shot against somebody's jaw. Then we were all on our feet again, stamping around on the grass, struggling like blind men.

"I got him!" Fox cried, but this was followed by an explosively landing punch that I just knew Fox couldn't have thrown (he simply could not have got that angry), and a moment later somebody hit the ground again. I dove at the guy and tore his shirt and got in another good punch in the face. But, whoever he was, he was tough. He went into a crouch and poured some more blows into my middle, and I could feel the breath pouring out of me again as I staggered back and fell over one of the tent stakes. I hit the ground pretty hard, and the next thing I knew I was looking up at the sky, gasping breathlessly.

They were struggling again, I could hear them panting.

"Hold him, Fox!" I yelled trying to get up. As I got shakily to my feet, my hand fell on a frying pan and, grasping it by the handle, I went back into the battle.

I swung out and promptly scored a hit on somebody's head as a metal bong rang out on the air. I heard Fox moan, and I knew I'd got the wrong man. I swung out again but missed. Then the other guy stepped in and hung one on my jaw that sent me spinning back and down again. Then I heard running. Fox was chasing him. I lay on the ground trying to collect my senses. Finally I reached into the tent for the flashlight, put it on and began sweeping it around.

"Fox!" I yelled.

For a few moments I didn't hear anything. Then I heard Fox call my name. I swung the light around and there he was, staggering back.

"What happened?" I asked.

He was holding his head.

"He got away," he said. "I thought I had him, but the next thing I knew I had run right into the river."

I saw now he was soaked, up to the knees. He came back and sat down. I lit our propane lantern and we looked at each other by the light.

"Who was it?" I asked.

"I don't know," he said feebly. His eyes didn't look too good.

"What do you think he was after?"

He shrugged. "Listen," he said, "you really clobbered me with something."

"The frying pan. I'm sorry, I thought I was hitting him."

"I'm glad to hear that. I was wondering whose side you were on." He took off his wet shoes and socks.

"You think it's safe to go to sleep?" I asked.

"Safe or not, I'm going. My head is spinning."

"You? Listen, I went down three times. In New York the referee would have stopped the fight."

He crawled into his sack and went to sleep. I sat there for a little while, trying to figure it all out. But I could hardly think. I just sat and watched the bugs swarming around the lantern. Then I put it out and went to sleep.

Camping sure was a lot of fun.

Chapter XI

First thing next morning we looked around to see if anything had been stolen. We took as complete an inventory as we could, but nothing seemed to have been taken. Also, we searched carefully to make sure nothing had been planted. The same person, or persons, who had framed Bruce might well have been trying to do the same to us. But we came up empty again. Nothing was gone, and the only thing added to the scene was the bump on Fox's head.

We fumbled through breakfast. We realized how badly we missed Bruce and needed him—not just as a friend but as a cook, too. Fox cooked the bacon so that it crackled and crumpled into crisp little crumbs when you touched it, like parchment that had been buried for three thousand years. I made the coffee, and it tasted like something that might have been drained out of a dead turtle. The scrambled eggs came out black for some reason. Only the toast tasted right.

After we cleaned up we went and sat by the river while we waited for Wilcie. Under normal circumstances, we would have been shoving off that morning. The passing water looked so inviting. I had grown to love canoeing this river in the short time I had been at it. There was such a fine, deep feeling in riding its

84

currents; even when running the rapids, when the water got rough and mean, you still knew it was simply challenging your skill, and the calm that came after the rapids was like a reward.

In the old days, when the fur trade was still in its early stages, there were men who hired themselves out as expert canoeists, taking the trappers and traders through the great rivers and silent lakes of Canada and the Far West. They were Frenchmen mostly and were called *voyageurs.* I'll bet they were men happy in their work.

Wilcie came by at nine thirty in her car.

"I had a fight with my father," she said. "He doesn't want me going around with you two. He thinks you're dangerous characters."

"Tell him he's wrong," I said. "Because we had a fight, too, and believe me, we're not very dangerous."

We told her about last night, about the stranger we had caught prowling around the camp and our brawl with him.

"Do you have *any* idea who it could have been?" she asked.

"Somebody tough," I said.

She looked sympathetically at the bump on Fox's head.

"Gee," she said, "he really hit you, didn't he?"

"My good friend did that," Fox said sourly.

"It was dark," I said. "I was trying my best."

"I was outnumbered, two to one," Fox said.

"Well, we know one thing for sure," she said. "It

had to be someone who knew you were away from the camp last night."

"In Anson," I said, "the way news travels, that takes in the whole town."

"And nothing is missing, nothing was taken?"

I shook my head.

"What's happening in town?" Fox asked.

"Everybody's talking about George Logan," she said. She was wandering around the camp. She picked up some of the still-warm coffee, sipped it, made a face and put it down. She did, however, swallow what she had sipped instead of spitting it out, which was a moral victory of sorts for us. "He's the big hero because he arrested Bruce," she said.

"He's a fool," Fox said. "I don't like him."

"Some of his friends are talking about him running for sheriff against Beeson in November," she said. "I'm sure he'd like to do that, too. So he said he'd sit for an interview this morning."

"You're going to interview him?" I asked.

"Right. Him and Garvin Delume both. We've got to stop speculating and get some hard facts. My editor says this is the most interesting thing to happen in Anson in years, and he wants to play it up. He wanted to do the interviews himself, but I begged him to let me have a crack at it." She paused then, staring at the ground. She had something on her mind, I could tell. Then she looked at us with a sort of embarrassed smile.

"Ironically," she said, "I have my father to thank

for being allowed to do the interviews. Do you know what he tried to do?"

"You don't have to tell us if you don't want to, Wilcie," I said. You could see she was upset by whatever it was her father had done, or tried to do.

"He went to Mr. Coleman—that's my boss, the editor—and offered him five hundred dollars if he would fire me. Can you imagine that?"

We didn't say anything. It was obvious that this hurt her deeply. It was truly a low thing for her father to have done. I guess it hurt her so much that she just had to talk about it.

"Mr. Coleman was so indignant that he almost threw my father out of the office. Then, just for spite, he told me I could run the interviews, which he had been planning to do himself."

"Why is your father so dead set against you working for the newspaper?" I asked.

"I don't know," she said. "I guess he just doesn't think it's woman's work."

"Or maybe he doesn't like you working on behalf of Bruce," Fox said.

"I don't know," she said.

We cleaned up the breakfast mess, tidied up a bit, then piled into Wilcie's car. On the way into town we stopped at the Delume house. Wilcie wanted to make sure Garvin was going to be in his office at the appointed hour. We pulled into the driveway, parked and got out of the car. The moment we did a big German shepherd came running and barking at us, galloping down the driveway. Fox and I got back into the car and slammed the doors. Wilcie stood there and greeted the dog, who turned out to be noisy but friendly. She roughed him up a bit and he seemed to love it.

"He's harmless," she said, shouting because we had rolled up the windows.

I rolled the window down.

"Fox is afraid of dogs," I said. "I just jumped in to keep him company."

Fox didn't say anything.

Wilcie walked to the house, the dog running ahead of her. We remained in the car.

"So?" I said.

"So what?" he asked.

"So nothing."

"Steven," he said, "you did the same thing last night."

"What same thing?"

"You said 'So?' and I asked 'So what?' and you said 'So nothing.' "

"I did?"

"Yes you did."

"So?"

"There, you did it again. For no good reason you sit there and say 'So?' "

"So what?" I asked him now.

"So nothing," he said and nodded his head at me with a single, firm, downward jerk.

"When there is no conversation going, it's socially polite to say 'So?' in order to get one going."

"If there is no conversation going," he said, "there's usually a good reason for it: there's nothing to be said. And particularly by me at the moment. I happen to be thinking. I'm trying to develop an idea in my head."

"A good one?"

He closed his eyes for a moment. When he opened them, he spoke firmly and evenly.

"If you will be still and let me think, I'll be able to find out."

I sat still and let him think. He did have an idea all right, but it wasn't until later that I would find out what it was.

Wilcie was back in a few minutes.

"He's in town," she said. "I spoke to the old lady."

"How is she?" Fox asked.

"She's all right. Moaning about her stolen jewels."

"Were they worth much?" I asked.

"Probably."

We rode into town. It was another bright, lovely day. It was so easy to lose yourself in all the natural beauty around you, from the blowing fields of flowers to the great wild mountains shouldering up against the blue sky . . . all of it carved out millions of years ago and left to dazzle the eye and sweep the mind of man. When you stop to consider the greatness of the mountains and the oceans, you realize you're not such a big shot. The only thing that makes man worthy of them, in my opinion, is his desire to conquer them.

So I occupied my mind with my daydreams while we rode into town, and Fox sat silently occupying his mind with his idea, whatever it was. Wilcie seemed puzzled by us.

"My, but the men from the East are quiet this morning," she said.

"It's a quiet day," I said.

"I think we're going to do something about that," she said.

Chapter XII

We arranged to meet in a couple of hours at the restaurant. Then Wilcie went off to her interviews while Fox and I went to the police station to visit Bruce. But first we wanted to have a few words with Sheriff Beeson.

He was in his office polishing a rifle when we walked in. We told him what had happened last night. He listened politely while we filled him in. We probably made it sound more dramatic than it was.

"This is a fine town you're running here, Sheriff," Fox said. "Why, a man isn't safe. Is this the way you treat strangers?"

"Any idea who it might have been?" Beeson asked.

"Do you?" Fox asked.

"No, sir. But I aim to investigate the matter. Do I have your permission to go out to your campsite and poke around?"

We couldn't very well say no since we had lodged the complaint. And anyway, there seemed no harm in it.

"Sure," Fox said. "You can go out there. But just be careful nobody jumps you."

"I carry a pistol, Mr. Huntington," Beeson said.

"There's good reason to," Fox said.

"I can understand your displeasure," Beeson said. "That's a mean bump you have there."

We didn't tell him how it had got there.

Then we went back to see Bruce. We had bought some magazines for him. When we got to his cell, however, we found that he already had some magazines, as well as some company.

It was Walt Pike. He was just leaving. He looked at us on his way out and mumbled something. Then he was gone.

"What did he want?" Fox asked Bruce.

"He said he'd come to apologize," Bruce said. "He brought me some magazines. He said he was sorry for the whole thing."

"He's got a guilty conscience," Fox said. "We figured it out last night after talking to him. *He's* the one who planted that diamond on you."

Bruce's eyes sharpened for a moment.

"Do you remember anything like that, anything remotely like that, when you were fighting with them?" I asked.

"It's possible," he said. "Of course it's possible. They were all over me . . . it could have been done. But why?"

"Somebody put him up to it," Fox said. "We don't know who yet."

"Have you told this to the man with the star?" Bruce asked.

"No," Fox said. "We don't have any definite proof

yet, so we can't say anything. But we're going to find out."

"Oh," Bruce said. You could see he didn't have much faith in our ability as detectives.

"Trust us," Fox asked.

Bruce nodded. He even tried to look hopeful, but it wasn't easy.

"Did Walt say much to you?" I asked.

"No, not about the brawl. Just that he was sorry. We mostly talked about New York, about life there. He was trying to be nice, I guess. He even asked me if I needed money, said he would give me some, if I needed it."

"I tell you he's got a heavy conscience," Fox said. "He's dying to get caught. It's a classic case of a guilty conscience." He had it all figured out. Big shot. Freshman psychology. Now it was all his idea.

"You fellows have been doing some heavy thinking," Bruce said. "Why, it's even raised a bump on your head there, Foxy."

Fox touched the spot.

"Clunkhead here hit me with a frying pan last night," he said.

Bruce laughed. "I knew the moment I was gone you two would fall apart."

Then we told him about the fight in the dark last night.

"I think you two boys ought to check in here with me," he said. "It's safer."

Then we handed him the magazines we had bought. They were the same ones Walt had given him. We couldn't seem to do anything right.

"Don't worry, Bruce," Fox said. "We're going to get you out of here soon. I'm working on a theory."

"Work hard," Bruce said. "I'm dying to get a canoe paddle back in my hands."

Then we left. When we were outside, I said, "I hope you're not giving him false hope."

"I'm not prepared to say at the moment," Fox said. He liked to be mysterious sometimes.

"I liked your theory about Walt Pike's guilty conscience," I said. "But it sounded like freshman psychology to me."

"Steven," he said, "the sign of a superior mind is one that is able to adapt to a good idea, even though that idea might have seemed foolish at first."

All right. I didn't say anything. You never know when a guy might be right.

We had some time to kill before we met Wilcie, so we wandered around town. There wasn't much wandering to do, of course; you walked a few blocks and you were out of town. There was a five-and-dime and a drugstore and a gun shop and of course a supermarket—that modern-day counterpart of the old general store.

There weren't many people around. The ones that we met seemed friendly enough, a few saying, "Howdy." We'd been around a few days now, and I guess they were getting used to us.

Then we were standing in front of Ackroy's barbershop. It was a small, narrow place, which you had to step up two concrete stairs to enter. We could see him in there behind his screen door, getting ready to shave somebody who was laid out in the barber chair under a white cloth like a corpse.

"You know," Fox said, "if there's one thing we ought to do above all else, it's straighten that guy out. What he tried to do—get his own daughter fired—is as low as you can get."

"You'd better be careful," I said. "He's got a razor in his hand."

"I'm not going to fight him. I just want to tell him what I think of him."

"Let's go," I said.

Ackroy looked up when we walked in. He had just begun to shave the customer, who was lying there with a face full of snowy white lather.

"What do you want?" Ackroy demanded.

"We just stopped by to tell you what we think of you," Fox said.

"And it isn't very good," I said.

"What you tried to do this morning was pretty low," Fox said.

The customer, who had been dozing, opened his eyes now and rolled them toward us. He couldn't move his head because Ackroy, who was about to begin shaving his upper lip, had taken hold of the man's nose and was still holding it.

"You guys better get out of here," Ackroy said.

95

"You should be ashamed of yourself," Fox said. "You might have ruined the career of a very promising newspaperwoman."

Ackroy was getting angrier. Without knowing he was doing it, he had begun pinching the nose of the man in the chair. The man began to wiggle his head around to try and loosen the grip. But Ackroy in his anger was holding on.

"If you guys don't get out of here," he said, "I'll call the law."

"Sure, why not?" Fox said. "In this town you can lock up a guy for anything. Well, you don't scare us, Mr. Ackroy. You're a bully and a bigot and a loud-mouth, but you don't scare us one bit."

Ackroy glared murderously at us. Then we heard a sort of squeaking noise, coming from the man in the chair.

"Let go my nose," the man said.

Ackroy looked down at him in astonishment, then let go. The man's nostrils popped out, they had been being squeezed so hard.

"I want you two to stay away from my daughter," Ackroy said, shaking the razor at us.

"They been bothering Wilcie?" the man in the chair asked. But Ackroy ignored him. A man lying on a barber chair with a face full of lather has very little impact on a situation.

"You're going to get that girl in trouble," Ackroy said. "It's dangerous for a young girl to go around investigating a crime."

"It's even more dangerous for somebody who's got something to hide," Fox said.

"We'll take care of Wilcie, don't worry," I said.

"There's been nothing but trouble since you guys came into town," Ackroy said.

"That's right," the man in the chair said. But he might just as well have been a dog barking in the night for all anybody listened to him.

"All the trouble has fallen on our heads," Fox said. "We're getting sick and tired of being pushed around."

"If you don't get out of my shop right now," Ackroy said, "you're going to be pushed around some more."

He was a pretty big guy, and he had that razor in his hand.

"All right," Fox said. "We're going. But you had better stop interfering in an official investigation."

"We're going to keep an eye on you," I said as we left.

We pushed open the screen door and let it slam back shut as we went out.

"I'm glad I got that off my chest," Fox said.

From inside the shop we heard the guy on the chair say, "Ouch! You nicked me."

I wouldn't want to be shaved by an angry barber.

Fox took my arm and led me away from the barbershop. We went into a side street and sat down on a bench there in front of an empty store.

We were both pretty depressed. I think more than anything else we were knocked down by how heartless

Ackroy had been about his own daughter, trying to get her bounced out of a job she loved so much.

"Can you imagine?" I said. "Him willing to pay five hundred dollars, too."

"Listen," Fox said, "where does he get that kind of money to throw around? You saw that place—a dinky little two-chair barbershop. Where does he come off being so reckless with five hundred dollars? And where does he get the money to send her to school, *and* buy her a car and things like that?"

"What are you driving at?" I asked.

"And I want to know why he's so hot to stop the investigation—which I think is what he's *really* got on his mind."

I didn't want to think about it. After all, this was Wilcie's father we were talking about. I didn't want to believe he was mixed up in this in any way; all he wanted was his daughter to stop associating with us. He did make the point that it could be dangerous for her, which was probably true. Also, considering his feelings toward blacks, you knew he didn't want his daughter taking any risks on behalf of Bruce. But one thing I knew for sure: that whatever Ackroy wanted, he wasn't going to get.

We killed some more time until Wilcie came back. We met her at noon in front of the restaurant. We were about to go in for some lunch and hear about Wilcie's interviews, when all of a sudden a kid about ten years old came running toward us with a message from Sheriff Beeson. He said the sheriff wanted to see us in his office. Right now.

Chapter XIII

When we walked into the police station we found Beeson there with Logan, the deputy. Logan had a kind of sour expression on his face, and my first guess was that Beeson had solved the crime and Logan was the guilty party. In fact I even had a fleeting image of Logan going into one cell while Bruce walked out of the other.

"I'm glad you're still in town," Beeson said when we all were assembled. "You'll be happy to know I've cleared up a little mystery for you."

We all looked at Logan. He was sitting on a chair, legs crossed, arms folded, looking anything but happy.

"Mr. Logan has a confession to make," Beeson said. When Logan didn't say anything, Beeson went on. "Well, at least he *had* a confession to make, and he made it. It was he who you fellows hassled with out at your campsite last night."

Logan nodded, to nobody in particular.

"I went out there this morning and had a look around," Beeson said. "I found this." He held up a piece of torn blue cloth no longer than your little finger. "One of you fellows tore his shirt in the fight. I knew George owned just such a shirt as this. Now, before you start jumping to any conclusions, let me tell you that when I asked him about it he said right out that he'd been there last night."

"But why?" I asked.

"He wasn't doing anything wrong, mind you," Beeson said. "He was looking for evidence."

"What kind of evidence?" Fox asked. "More diamonds?"

Now Logan spoke up.

"The possibility existed," he said. "If your friend had one diamond, why couldn't you two have the rest of the stuff?"

It was crazy and insulting and slanderous, of course; but at the same time, given his turn of mind, Logan was not entirely wrong. He had made one arrest, got a lot of glory, and was out to make a clean sweep of it. He was dead wrong in his figuring, but you couldn't honestly fault what he had done. Except for one thing.

"Why didn't you tell us who you were?" I asked.

Logan didn't answer. Beeson did.

"Because he had asked me yesterday afternoon if he could go out and search your campsite. I told him no."

"Why, Jim?" Wilcie asked.

"Because I didn't think there was anything to find. So he went on his own and felt kind of foolish when you fellows caught him. He'd seen you riding off with Wilcie and figured the coast was clear. So he hiked out there and started poking around. He was just plain embarrassed about letting you know who he was, being such a top-flight investigator who got caught in the act," Beeson said, giving Logan a sly look.

Logan looked unhappier than ever. He knew this was going to find its way into the newspaper. Not only had he gone and disobeyed orders, but his big move had backfired on him. And as soon as we proved Bruce innocent, then even his big arrest would turn to vapor.

"Well," I said, "he might not be Sherlock Holmes, but he packs a pretty good wallop in either hand."

"Oh, he's efficient at certain things," Beeson said. "He's welcome to stay on as deputy as long as he wants—just so he doesn't go off conducting his own investigations."

Logan just sighed. I felt kind of sorry for him. No matter how big a fool a man is, you don't like to see him strung out like that in front of people. When somebody who deserves it finally gets what's coming to him, it's always better to hear about it than see it.

Then we went out.

"Beeson is a good cop," Wilcie said as we headed back toward the restaurant. "Except that he's lazy."

"I agree," Fox said. "He should be out poking around. Why isn't he grilling Walt Pike?"

"Oh, he wouldn't get anything out of Walt. We got more out of him than Beeson could have got in a year."

"Do you know Walt went to see Bruce and offered him money?" I said.

"No, I didn't," Wilcie said. "But you see, that's his

conscience at work. I think if we waited long enough he would finally walk in and tell the whole story. But we can't wait."

"Especially Bruce can't wait," I said.

Over lunch she told us about her interviews. First she'd seen Logan. He told her his version of the story. Garvin Delume had called to report the theft. Garvin also mentioned that there were three strangers camping down at the river and that one of them was black. So when Bruce walked into town, Logan felt it quite natural to bring him in for interrogation, then to search him. Bruce had told him about being roughed up by Walt and his friends, but once the diamond was found nothing else seemed to matter.

"Did you find out what Logan was doing that morning?" I asked.

"Yes. He was around town the whole time. He had breakfast, then went to the hardware store and hung around. He couldn't have taken the jewelry. And anyway, if he had, he needn't have gone through the trouble of arranging anything with Walt and his friends. He could just as easily have slipped it into Bruce's pocket while searching him."

I hated to lose my favorite suspect, especially one who had knocked me down three times, one who had been so dead sure Fox and I were involved with the theft he had come in the dark to search our belongings.

"I still think he could be involved," I said. Stubborn.

"No," Wilcie said. "You have to remember another thing. We're looking for someone who would steal jewelry for the good old reason: they need the money. Now, I know the people around here better than you do. George Logan isn't a rich man, but he's a reasonably content one. He's happy in his work; he loves being a deputy. When he's not on duty he just sits around and talks with the boys. He's a very simple man, with a nice wife and a happy home life. As far as I can see, he doesn't need money badly enough to take such a chance."

"Then who needs money around here?" I asked. "Give us the list."

"Steve," Fox said, "please be still and let Wilcie finish."

"I'm trying to make a constructive contribution," I said.

"You failed," Fox said.

While we ate our sandwiches and drank our coffee, Wilcie went on. Her second interview was with Garvin Delume, in his office. Yesterday Delume had not been in his office, but had stayed home to work on a painting. He was in his studio near the house working on a picture, when he heard his mother scream. He immediately ran to the house, where he learned that the jewelry was missing. It was quickly established that the theft had to have occurred that morning, since the old lady insisted that nothing had been disturbed when she had gotten up. The old lady went out into the garden and puttered around for a while. When she went back to her room some time later, she saw the jewelry box open and the contents gone.

Garvin Delume told Wilcie that he had seen us setting up camp the day before while hiking. So the first thing he thought after the robbery was that we were involved. He immediately called the police, getting Logan on the phone (Sheriff Beeson was not there at the time). Delume admitted being surprised when he learned that Bruce had walked into town soon after. He would have thought, Delume said, that Bruce would have seen to it that we were back on the river as soon as possible.

"I don't like his story," Fox said when Wilcie was through.

"Why?" I asked.

"It's too neat. Everything is packaged too tightly. The boys waiting for Bruce—almost as if they knew it would be he passing—and then Bruce walking into town and that deputy virtually waiting there for him."

"But Delume couldn't have known Bruce would be the one going to town," I said.

"Then he didn't care; he was gambling on one of us walking into town. He must know that's a popular campsite—no doubt people have stopped there before, and as a rule one of them will walk in to buy some supplies. It was Bruce's bad luck to be the one to go to town."

"But why would Delume steal his own jewelry?" I asked.

"I don't know," Fox said. "I don't know anything, except that there's something about his story that stinks to high heaven. I'll bet anything *he's* got that jewelry."

"Where?" Wilcie asked. I could see she was getting interested in Fox's idea.

"Right there in the house."

"The old lady might find it," she said.

"Then somewhere else, where she wouldn't go."

"His studio," Wilcie said.

"Right," Fox said. "That would be the place."

I could see it all. You get involved in these things and sooner or later *you're* the one doing something illegal. I knew just what they were thinking. It was in the air, in their faces. They—we—were going to break into Garvin Delume's studio that night to look for the jewelry. I think I saw the idea take hold of them even before they did. Fox was excited because he was so sure he was right, and Wilcie because she obviously was the kind of girl who would climb into a dragon's nose just for the excitement.

"All right," I said, even before either of them got off another word. "Where and what time do we meet?"

Chapter XIV

Ten thirty at night was the time, the dirt road near the campsite was the place. It was a short walk from there to the Delume house. Fox and I were standing there in the night, in a chill wind that was blowing down from the mountains, rustling the cottonwoods and cedars and all those other trees the names of which Bruce knew. Never in my life had I felt more like a fugitive, a criminal—and I hadn't even done anything yet.

All afternoon, all evening, I had begged Fox not to go through with it. It was crazy, dangerous, and illegal, I told him. I even drew a picture for him of Logan catching us: just think how evilly delighted Logan would be, since he had suspected us all along and since we had made him look foolish. But nothing would budge him. Fox can become as stubborn as a mule when he wants.

"If you don't want to come," he said, "nobody will hold it against you."

"Except that I won't be able to paddle that canoe alone with you and Bruce in jail."

"Stay out of it. I don't care," he said.

But he knew I wouldn't, and I knew I wouldn't. For one thing, he knew how I felt about Wilcie, that I wouldn't dream of playing chicken in front of her. And for another thing, suppose Fox was right and they did find something? How would I feel being left out of it?

So there we were, standing in the dark. It was so quiet we could hear the river faintly, going its way. We should have stayed on it, I was thinking. Never stopped here. Bruce wouldn't be in jail; we wouldn't be standing here about to become housebreakers, or studio-breakers. But then I wouldn't have met Wilcie. But she had a boyfriend. No doubt some nitwit football player who they had to lead around the campus on a chain. No, she wouldn't go for that type. She obviously had better taste. But if she had such good taste, then why didn't she go for me? But if she didn't go for me, then at least she wasn't going for Fox. That would have been too much.

Then we saw her headlights. My last hope was gone. I had even been on her father's side, hoping the fat bigot would take some action and tie her up or something. But no. Here she was, and we were going to have to go through with it.

The car pulled up to us and stopped. She turned off the headlights, and it was all very mysterious. She got out, holding a flashlight.

"All set?" she asked.

"Are we sure we want to do this?" I asked.

"Steve is afraid," Fox said.

"I'm not afraid," I said. "I just want to be sure the plan is solid."

107

"There's no plan," Fox said. "We just slip around behind the house and break into the studio."

"That sounds solid," I said.

"He's afraid," Fox said.

If I had been holding the frying pan, I would have raised another knob on his head.

"Don't be foolish," I said, trying to be cool. "It's Wilcie I'm concerned about."

"Steve, you're sweet," she said. "I appreciate your thoughtfulness." Even in the dark I could see her bright smile. That alone was worth risking jail for.

"Are you really engaged?" I asked.

"Steven," Fox said impatiently, "you can discuss Wilcie's personal life later. Right now there's something more important at hand."

Okay.

So we headed for the Delume house. We walked slowly. We *all* were a bit nervous. It was quite dark; the moon was buried under heavy, quiltlike layers of clouds. The wind kept blowing, and it seemed to me there was a smell of rain. When we reached the Delume grounds, the wind was very strong and you could hear the trees tossing with great rustling sounds, filling the night. As we entered the driveway the house came into view; there was but one light on, in an upstairs room that Wilcie said was Garvin's.

We were about halfway down the driveway when the dog started to bark. It was at once a welcome and an unwelcome sound to my ears: welcome because with any good sense we should have retreated then and there, and unwelcome because, if we didn't retreat,

108

the barking was likely to alert Delume and that would mean trouble.

"Stand still," Wilcie said, letting the dog come to us.

The big shepherd stopped barking the moment he saw it was Wilcie. He grew playful and jumped up and put his front paws on her, and she took his face in her hands and roughed him up a bit, all the while whispering to him what a good dog he was.

A face appeared in the upstairs window for a moment, no doubt brought there by the barking, but then it went away. The dog stayed quiet and in fact soon disappeared back into the night. We waited for about five minutes, just in case the barking had made Delume suspicious. Then we moved on. We slipped around the house and headed for the studio. It was a few hundred feet behind the house, in a wooded area. We followed a path out to it.

The studio was built of logs, except for one whole side which was glass. That wasn't so good, since we were going to be poking around in there with a flashlight, which could be easily seen—if somebody happened to look that way.

The door was locked, but the lock gave easily under my sturdy shoulder. We went inside, closing the door behind us. Immediately we were struck by the smell of paint and turpentine. In the dark we could see canvases scattered around. When Wilcie turned on the flashlight, the beam began picking up the different paintings. They were mostly of nature scenes, things like trees and mountains and flowers. They looked pretty amateurish to me.

"This could take all night," I said.

There seemed to be a million cans and tubes and envelopes and jars and drawers, any number of places where a handful of jewelry could be hidden. I think even Fox was discouraged, though he pretended not to be.

"We'll find them," he said.

Now that we were there I could see how crazy the whole thing was, that we had been carried there by a momentary enthusiasm that had got out of hand, the whole thing based on Fox's hunch. There was still time to get out, but I wasn't going to be the one to suggest it.

So we began looking around, opening drawers and cabinets, looking into cans of paint and envelopes, moving canvases around. It surely was going to take hours, since we had only the one flashlight and could look only where it shone instead of splitting up, with each of us taking a corner.

Then suddenly something hit the window, like a scattering of pebbles, and we all froze. We quickly realized what it was, however. It had begun to rain, all at once. We listened to it pound against the roof and the glass wall. It made the whole thing spookier, what with the darkness closing right in on wherever the light had been.

We kept searching. It all seemed so hopeless. We didn't even know for sure if Delume had taken the stuff (much less why: why should a wealthy man swipe his mother's jewelry?) and, if he had, where he had put it. He had that big house, as well as all of the outdoors in which to hide it. So why here?

"If he took them, they'll be here," Wilcie said, as if she had been reading my thoughts. "This is his place. Nobody is ever allowed in here, not even his mother."

"Temperamental artist," Fox said, opening a cabinet while Wilcie held the light fixed on the shelves within.

"His paintings are dogs, if that's any consolation," I said.

"Steve took an art appreciation course last semester," Fox said. "He's able to tell Rembrandt from Norman Rockwell."

"I learned a lot in that course, boy," I said. "I'd recommend it strongly to old Van Gogh Delume."

"Do you paint?" Wilcie asked.

"I dabble," I said.

"Once he cut his finger and put some iodine on," Fox said. "That's the extent of his work."

"It stopped the bleeding," I said. I was such a lousy painter that black paint turned pale at the sight of my brush. But that was no reason for him to bring it up in front of Wilcie.

We kept looking. But nothing. Nothing. Nothing. We couldn't find a thing. It was discouraging. We lifted the cushion out of the easy chair that was in the studio and slid our hands into the padding. Nothing. We looked under and behind everything. Nothing. The rain continued to pour. Occasionally the light flashed across the big window and we could see the rain-smeared glass.

111

And then the sound of the rain suddenly got louder, the noise seemed to be filling the place up. And then I realized the wind was blowing on me. We all felt it and whirled around. The door was open. Somebody was standing there. A moment later a flashlight blazed brightly in our faces.

Chapter XV

"What are you doing here?"

It was Garvin Delume. There was real anger in his voice. We were trying to shield our eyes from the bright glare of his flashlight, which really packed a lot of candle-power.

"What are you doing here?" he asked again, the rain pouring behind him.

I don't think it was just that we were trespassing on his property, but that we were in this particular place, his studio, which was his special, private place. We had violated something that was very personal to him.

"If you'll put down your light, we'll talk to you," Fox said.

The light remained fixed on us for another few moments, then was lowered. Wilcie had her flashlight aimed at the floor, but the light splashed far enough to dimly show Garvin Delume standing in the door-way. He was wearing a long raincoat and a floppy rain-hat. The flashlight in his hand, which he kept down but did not turn off, looked as if it were a foot long.

"I demand to know what you're doing here," Delume said.

It was a fair enough question, any way you looked at it. Only I didn't have an answer. And for once Wilcie didn't have the answer. The tension built, with

Delume standing in the doorway with the wind and rain at his back, both his and Wilcie's flashlights flaring against the floor. And then Fox spoke out. Not only did he speak out but he told a lie. And not only was it a lie, but it was the biggest, most smashing lie you ever heard. And not only that, but it came from a guy who simply did not tell lies.

"We're here," Fox said, "because Walt Pike told us you paid him to rough up Bruce Price and plant that diamond in his pocket."

The lie was so incredible that it made me dizzy for a moment. It must have done something to Delume too, because he didn't say anything for a time, just continued to stand there. I had expected anything but that: an expression of disbelief, an angry denial, a horse-laugh. But there was only the silence.

Then Delume closed the door behind him, shutting out the noise of the rain. He turned on a light. The rain was running off the brim of his hat, and he took it off now and put it down. He turned off his flashlight and sighed. Then he sat down on a wooden folding chair and shook his head.

"All right," he said. "It was a mad, foolish scheme. I knew that from the beginning. And I'm sorry. I'm truly sorry."

Nobody said anything. We simply didn't know what to say. We had stumbled right into it, into the explanation for the whole thing, and none of us knew what to say.

"What made the boy tell?" he asked. "Oh, it doesn't make any difference. In a way it's just as well. I hated to think about that black fellow in jail for something he didn't do . . . even though I knew from the beginning that that was just where they'd put him."

"Why did you need a scapegoat?" Fox asked. "Why not just claim the jewelry was stolen?"

"I would have run the risk of not being believed by my mother," Delume said. "She knew I needed money. I had to have someone to blame it on."

"Tell us, Mr. Delume," Fox said. "How did you know Bruce would be walking on the road yesterday morning?"

Delume looked up at us now. He had a weak, sickly smile.

"You told me," he said.

"I did?" Fox said.

"The three of you did, in your tent, two nights ago. I was frankly uneasy when I heard you were camping there, so I decided to go down and see what I could see. I didn't see much, but I heard you talking in your tent."

I snapped my fingers.

"Then it was you we heard in the dark," I said. I turned to Fox. "Remember we heard something . . . we thought it might be a bear?"

"I'm afraid it was something more dangerous," Delume said, with that weak smile again.

"So you heard Bruce say he would be going into town in the morning," Fox said.

"Yes," Delume said. "You made some joke about a black man going into town, so I knew it would be he."

"So you called Walt Pike," Fox said.

"I called him in the morning. I knew he was a boy ripe for mischief and that, since he wasn't working, he could stand some money. Also, I had heard that there had almost been some trouble between him and the black fellow, so I knew he'd probably go along with it. I told him to gather some of his friends. I promised him fifty dollars to do what he did."

"Were the others in on it?" I asked.

"No," Delume said. "I left the diamond in a place where Walt could pick it up, which he did without the others noticing. Then they laid back and waited for your friend. It was all so simple."

"When did you take the jewelry?" Wilcie asked.

"In the morning. I didn't upset anything, so my mother didn't suspect. Then, just before calling the police, I moved some things about in her room, knowing that would make her suspicious and discover the 'theft.' The rest went so easily according to plan it was ridiculous."

The rain had slackened somewhat, was now falling in a light, steady drumming.

"So there," Delume said. "There you have it, the whole story."

"Not quite," Wilcie said. "You've left something out. You haven't told us why you did this. Frankly, Mr. Delume, none of it makes sense."

"It does to me," he said.

"But you must have had a reason," she said. "You're such a wealthy man."

"But I'm not," he said quickly. "My mother is the wealthy one."

"Do you mean to say you did it because you really needed money?" I asked.

"The jewelry was insured; also, it would fetch a good deal of money through a person of rather questionable character that I know in Denver."

"But why should you need money?" Wilcie asked.

He didn't say anything.

"Mr. Delume," she said, "I've known you all my life. I know you're a good and decent man, and to have done something like this is unlike you. I can assure you none of us hold anything against you. You've been honest so far, you've told us the truth. Now tell us the rest of it. Perhaps we can help you."

He sat silent for at least two full minutes, which is a lot longer than it sounds. Then he began nodding his head, as if agreeing to something with himself. He looked at Wilcie, as if he were going to say something pleasant.

"I'm being blackmailed," he said. "I've been being blackmailed for years. Bled white."

"By whom? For what?"

Now he seemed pained, a most distressed look crossing his face.

"May I tell you?" he asked.

We held still.

"Yes, maybe I should, at last," he said. He seemed to listen to the rain for a moment, looking at the glass wall where it was streaming. "It goes back a long time, you see," he said, "to when my father was just launching his business, buying land with his partner, Jack Evers. One weekend they decided to do some hunting and went off together into the mountains. It was in the fall, just before the snows. There was an accident. Jack stumbled and accidentally shot himself. He was in serious need of medical attention."

"But I heard—" Wilcie started to say.

"Yes, I know. You heard what everyone did. That Jack Evers and my father separated, planning to meet later at Great Horn Creek. That was what my father told everyone. That they planned to meet and Jack Evers never showed up. You heard that my father came into town and a search party was organized and that they scoured the mountains for days and never found Jack. But the truth is Jack shot himself out near Maxwell Canyon—the opposite direction from which my father led the search party."

"But why?" Wilcie asked.

"Why? Because they were partners in a business that was going to do very well. My father was a shrewd real-estate man. And their partnership was informal, in that there were no papers. So when Jack Evers was declared dead, leaving no heirs, my father naturally took over the whole thing. You know what happened after that. He made a fortune."

"But if they were alone out there," Wilcie said, "how could anyone have known about it?"

"Because my father made one mistake. He never went back and properly disposed of the body. He couldn't face doing that, I guess. And anyway, he probably felt that the body was in a place so out of the way that no one would ever find it, and even if they did, years later, so what? Jack simply got lost, shot himself, and that was that. And in due time someone did find the body. But he also found something else. A diary. Once he realized what my father had done, Jack wrote down the truth in a small leather-bound notebook he had with him. It was found carefully wrapped—he wanted to make sure the elements didn't destroy it. I've seen pages from it. Oh, I've seen them all right. And I've been paying for it ever since."

Delume sat quietly for a few moments. We watched him, not saying anything. The rain was beating lightly upon the roof and against the window.

"I've never told my mother about this," he said. "It would have broken her heart. She and my father were . . . a devoted couple. So for years my father paid, and after he died I paid. I've *been* paying. You can't ever satisfy a blackmailer you know, you have to keep feeding him forever. He always comes for one last handout. I'd finally used up all of my personal money and so had to do this thing with the jewelry in order to raise more. I simply could not go to my mother for it. She'd given me sums from time to time, but she was getting suspicious. She wouldn't give me any more without knowing exactly what it was for."

"So you threw it on Bruce's head," Fox said.

"I did a terrible thing, sir," Delume said. "I played upon the prejudices of people. I knew a black person wouldn't have a chance. Not a chance."

119

"Oh, Mr. Delume," Wilcie said. "I feel so sorry for you."

"Thank you, young lady. And since you do, I'm going to return the favor."

"What do you mean?" she asked.

Fox said it. "He means the person who's been blackmailing him is your father."

Her eyes widened. She stared at Delume, not wanting to believe it until he confirmed it. He nodded gently.

No wonder Ackroy had been so fast with a five-hundred-dollar bribe offer to Wilcie's boss. No wonder he wanted Wilcie to stop poking around into this thing—he had probably figured it out for himself.

"I hope you're getting a good education at that college," Delume said ruefully. "I've been paying for it."

"I'll pay it back, Mr. Delume," Wilcie said softly. "All of it. I swear."

"I've never held it against you," Delume said. "Years ago a wrong was committed, and not by you or by me. Through it my father accumulated a great deal of money, and I benefited from that, and you've been benefiting from that. But eventually that small cry of justice must be heard."

"Mr. Delume," Fox said, "will you come with us now and tell this to Sheriff Beeson?"

"Yes," Delume said. "It's about time we threw open the windows and let in the fresh air."

120

Chapter XVI

We went straight to the police station, right then and there, piling into Delume's car and driving through the rain. When we got there, we found Beeson sitting in his office with his feet up on the desk, reading a detective novel.

"You can open up those golden gates and let Bruce out," I said when we walked in.

Wilcie then proceeded to tell him the story. You could see the disbelief in Beeson's face, and whenever she came to another particular twist in the tale Beeson's eyes would shoot to Delume and the latter would sadly nod that it was true. Wilcie told all of it, right down to the blackmailing activities of her father. This last part wasn't easy for her, but she got it said.

You could see the surprise and the confusion in Beeson's face. Here was a man who hadn't been faced with any serious crime in a long time, now suddenly getting a load of it thrown into his lap all at once. He was going to have to sort out between false accusation, conspiracy, blackmail and probably some other things, too, that only a sharp-headed lawyer like Fox's father could figure out.

"How much of this has to become public?" Wilcie asked.

"That depends," Beeson said.

"All of it," Delume said. He looked at Wilcie. "I'm sorry," he said. "I owe you a great debt, but nevertheless it's all got to come out: the sins of my father, your father, and myself."

Beeson didn't say anything. I knew what he was thinking: the moment Bruce walked out of jail George Logan lost his big arrest. Not only that, but he had arrested the wrong man. This meant he wouldn't be running against Beeson for sheriff.

"Charges could be lodged against you for giving the police false information, Mr. Delume," Beeson said.

"Sheriff," Delume said, "while we're standing here talking about what might or might not happen to me, the minutes are ticking by and an innocent man is sitting in a jail cell. Let's concern ourselves with him, shall we?"

We all went back to where the cells were. Bruce was asleep on the cot. For no good reason—I was so excited, I guess—I let out the loudest whistle you ever heard, and he wakened with a look of shock. Who knows what a sleeping man is dreaming about in a jail cell?

"You're free, Mr. Price," Beeson said, sticking a big key into the cell door.

Bruce stood up slowly. Then he tucked in his shirt. He didn't say a word, didn't ask a question. After all, he was an innocent man. He walked out slowly as Beeson swung open the door, with a look of deep pride, not even of relief or satisfaction, but this calm, quiet pride, as if to say, "I've always been free."

After all, he was an innocent man.

Delume drove us back. Wilcie got into her car and went home. I didn't envy her. There was going to be quite a scene there when she faced her father with the story of the blackmail. And poor Delume was going to have to go home and break the news to his mother that her beloved husband had had the soul of a murderer. And George Logan was going to learn that he was no longer a hero. And so on.

It was past midnight when we got back to camp. We all were bushed. Bruce was for launching the canoe right then and there, in the rain and the dark, and going down the river. He was only kidding, of course, but it showed how anxious he was to get away from there. And who could blame him?

We crawled into the tent and into our sacks. The rain kept beating lightly on the roof of the tent.

"Fox," I said, "I have to ask you something."

"Ask me tomorrow," he said.

"Bruce," I said, "I have to ask you something too."

"Ask me tomorrow," he said.

I took the hint and closed my eyes. I fell asleep listening to the rain falling on our tent and in the grass and in the rolling river and over the great mountains. It sounded comfortable, even cozy. I guess it always sounds better when things are good.

* * *

It was gone in the morning. The rain, I mean. The sky had cleared and the sun was up, shining brightly on the moist grass and trees.

Bruce made us a good breakfast (his cooking tasted better than ever now); then we began to break camp. We cleaned up, packed and got ready to shove off. We took our time at it because Wilcie said she'd be there to say good-bye. We were ready to go at eight thirty, and by nine she still wasn't there. The canoe was all packed and we were just sitting around.

Then she showed up.

"I had to stop off at the Delumes'," she said. "I gave them the diary. I watched them burn it. The old lady never said a word. It was a very sad scene."

"How about your father?" I asked.

She shrugged.

"He's sulking," she said. "He knows he's been doing wrong. What will happen, I don't know. I just don't know. He could go to jail for blackmail. Delume could go to jail for falsely reporting a crime. A lot of things could happen."

"Listen," I said, "now that we're all here, I want to know something." I turned to Fox. "What made you tell Delume that lie last night? That was the most outrageous thing I ever heard."

Fox was so proud of himself. He put his hands into his pockets and rocked back on his heels for a moment.

"It was simple deductive reasoning," he said. "I first

began to get suspicious when we drove into Delume's driveway that first time—when his dog came barking at us. I wondered why, if a stranger had come onto the grounds and into the house, why the dog hadn't barked. No one ever mentioned the dog barking. So it stood to reason that the thief had to be someone the dog knew—namely, its owner. The second thing was when Bruce told us Walt Pike had offered him money. Now, since we were told Walt was out of work, where would he have got the money from? I took a chance and put it together, that's all."

"That was brilliant, Fox," Wilcie said.

"Thank you," Fox said with a little bow. I felt like kicking him.

"When you accused Delume of paying Walt to plant the diamond, I almost died," Wilcie said.

"A calculated risk," Fox said. "Except that I was certain I was on firm ground."

All right, all right. I was getting bored with how brilliant Fox was. He had guessed, that's all.

"It was a good guess," I said.

"It was more than a guess," he said. "I used logic."

Wilcie was smiling. She could see I was jealous.

"Are you really getting engaged?" I asked.

"Yes," she said.

Oh.

Then we were all looking at Bruce.

"I know what you want," he said.

"Will you tell us?" Wilcie asked.

"But it's my secret," he said with a smile.

"It will be safe," she said.

He looked up at the mountains, the sky; you could *feel* him feeling the wonders around him, the majesty, the great, strong beauty that was part of time and nature. Then he looked at Wilcie.

"I guess I can tell you," he said. "After all, I owe you a lot." Now he looked at me. "What was I doing for an hour and fifteen minutes?" He smiled. "Well, I'll tell you. After I had finished with those boys I kept walking toward town. On the way I saw this beautiful field of flowers. So I went into it. I walked around and around, just staring, smelling the air. And I picked myself a bouquet."

"But why didn't you tell?" I asked.

Bruce put his strong black hand on my shoulder.

"First of all," he said, "I wouldn't have been believed. And second of all, I know how some people think. What would they have said when they heard that the big strong black man had been picking flowers? So I left my flowers by the roadside when I got to town, meaning to pick them up later. But, I tell you, man, I wasn't going to sit in any jail and tell any policeman that I'd been picking flowers."

I understood. I think we all did. It was something you're able to feel more than explain.

We said our good-byes then.

"I'm going to miss you all," Wilcie said. "You were all the fun."

"Come East," I said. "We have lots of fun there all the time."

"Maybe on my honeymoon," she said.

I guess she really was getting engaged.

We put the canoe in the water, then took our places, Fox in the bow, Bruce in the middle, me in the stern, paddles in hand. The river was calm here and we paddled out into the middle where the current picked us up.

When I looked back Wilcie was standing on the shore waving to us. I waved back. Then I looked ahead, at the sun shining on the bright water and at the canyon walls. The wind was in my face and it felt good. According to the map there were rapids a few miles ahead, and who knew what else?

The Author

Donald Honig is the author of the popularly received *Dynamite!*, published last year by Putnam's. The author of 15 novels and 150 short stories, Mr. Honig now makes his home in New York City.